# Legends of Love

## THE ANGELIC KINGDOM

Other Titles by

RONNIE SMITH

*The Last White Ruby*

*The Royal Princess and the Three Magical Gifts*

*Roses for the Most High*
*Poetry Celebrating the Mystical Christian Path*

*The Sky is for Wonder*

*Deployed Flight and Sometimes Eternity*

*Mystic Land and Celtic Saints*

*Spanish Roses*
*Poetic Revelation of the Spanish Mystics*

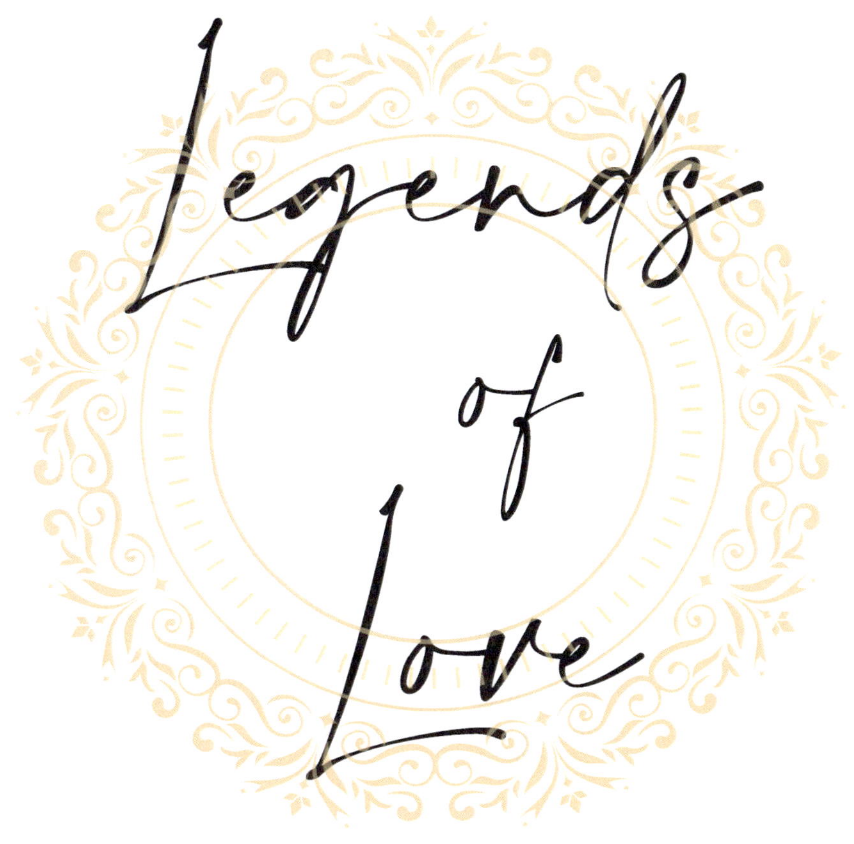

# Legends of Love

## THE ANGELIC KINGDOM

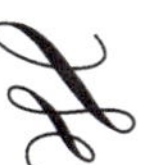

# RONNIE SMITH

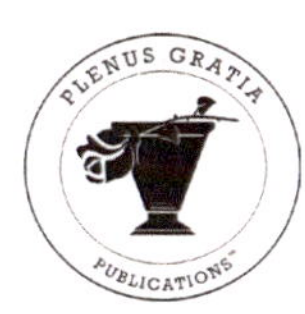

PLENUS GRATIA PUBLICATIONS

For information about this title or to order other books and/or electronic media, contact the publisher:

Ronnie Smith/Plenus Gratia Publications®
PlenusGratiaToday@gmail.com

Cover and interior design by The Book Cover Whisperer:
OpenBookDesign.biz

Legends of Love, The Angelic Kingdom /Ronnie Smith. —1st ed.

979-8-9924306-0-8 Paperback
978-1-7356595-9-6 Hardcover
979-8-9924306-1-5 eBook

Printed in the United States of America

FIRST EDITION

*This book is devoted to the eternal love of*
*Mary, the Blessed Mother*

CONTENTS

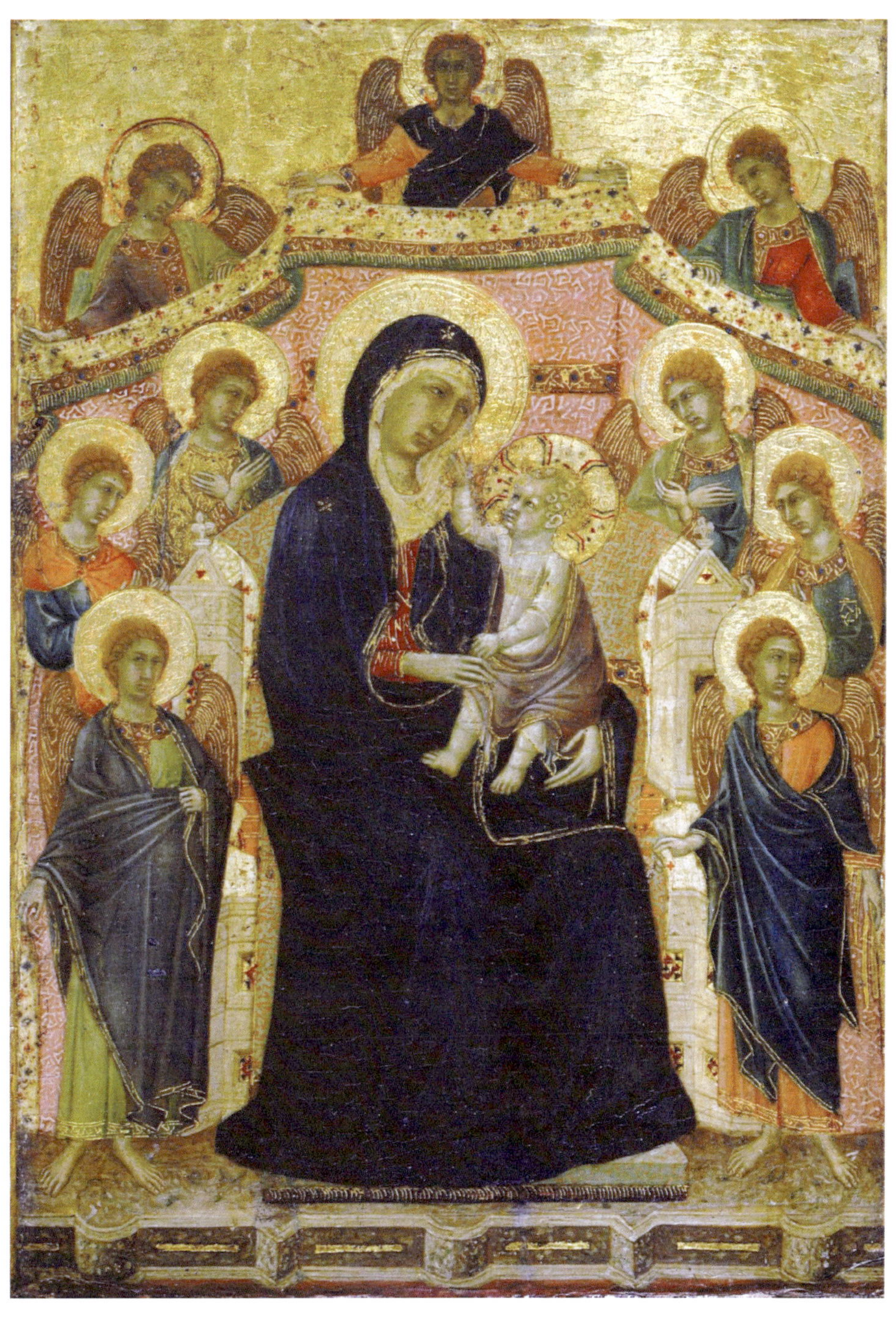

[1] *Diptych with Engaged Moldings*, (Poplar, gilt), 1310-25 (Siena, Italy), Robert Lehman Collection, 1975, Courtesy Metropolitan Museum of Art, New York, CC0.

# ACKNOWLEDGMENTS

I would like to recognize the people who were part of this growth in awareness that inspired, supported, and encouraged this work which enabled and at times consoled me to bring it to fruition: the clergy and religious throughout my entire faith journey, Kathleen Sweeney, Matthew Smith, Ken Merryman, Joyce Wingfield, my holy spiritual family, Vicki Smith the healer, and the holy angelic kingdom.

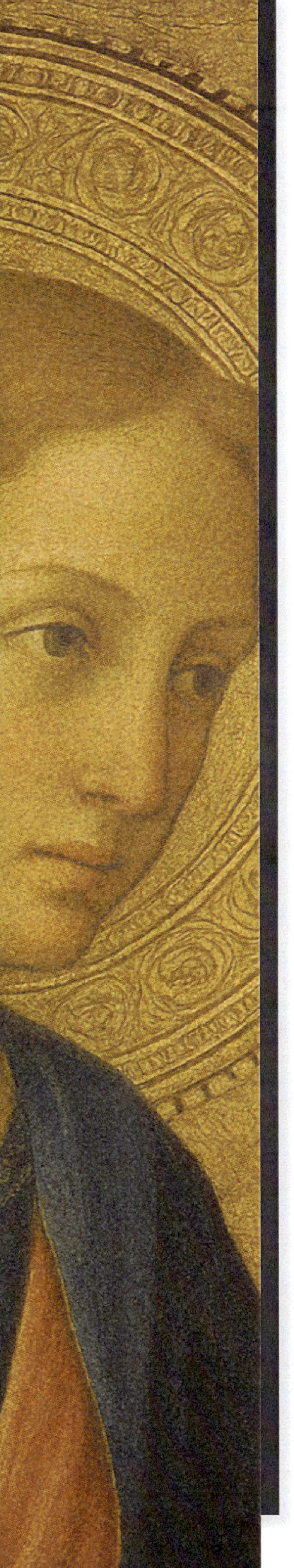

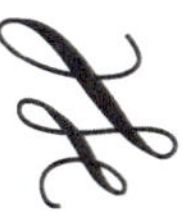

# INTRODUCTION

*"Are they (Angels) not all ministering spirits sent to serve,*
*for the sake of those who are to inherit salvation?"*
*(Hebrews 1:14)*

After writing some books centered on the mystic saints of the Christian Church, I wondered about a book focusing on the angelic hierarchy. This idea, connected to the saints, would be to endeavor to build along the lines of God's plan, two hierarchies united by one divine province. Intuition said it was possible, yet difficult. Christianity is founded on the supernatural and how it intersects with this physical world. I found in my Christian experience that the angels are not only part of the story of Christianity, but they are a fact of life, active in the physical and non-physical worlds. The modern world, contemplative religious orders notwithstanding, tends to ignore angels due to the West's imbalanced focus on gross materiality. This perspective creates a disparity between mysticism, asceticism, and the objective approach to express love for God through religion. We do pay attention to the Christmastime stories of the angels who guided the Holy Family, and who heralded the birth of Jesus. Some Western cultures such as the Celts, describe matter-of-factly the influential stories of angelic spirits who guided the lives of their saints. So this book has hopes to spread abroad the knowledge a little further about our brothers of the angelic hierarchy and to enunciate the divine wisdom and beauty which they bring to us, humanity, as they contribute to the complex architecture of our tiny part of the Cosmos (Creation).

Due reverence is proffered in this book for the contributions of knowledge from other religious cultures, most much older than Christianity, which I as a college student started studying under tutelage at Loyola Maryland. This is a conscious attempt to demonstrate inclusiveness and refute the heresy of separateness. May this book, then, encourage the spiritual man and woman. After all, every soul on Earth has a guardian angel, revealing that all belong in the plan of God.

It should be stated that the First Principle of the divine angelic hierarchy is union. All is One. Angelic origin and human origin are from the same uncreated Logos. We are family and offspring from the same Creator. It follows that the Divine Will of the Logos promulgates the Plan of Creation. The spiritual/human and the celestial/angelic hierarchies are to execute that plan, and in the process grow in holiness. The foundation of this book is necessarily Christian because of my path through Catholicism, but it applies to all of Christianity and more. Mystical Christianity is universal to all humanity. The Christ gives the sons and daughters of God the path to eternal life. The angelic kingdom presents a facet of eternal life that awaits all who choose to rise from the dust of this world.

To sense the whole, there are many references to the angelic kingdom in the religions and wisdom traditions throughout the world. The angels are referred to as *devas* (from Sanskrit) in the East, and different names color their varied ranks and statuses throughout Judaism, Buddhism, Zoroastrianism, and Hinduism, etc. Throughout the Christian Bible, there are approximately 270 references to angels depending on the version of the text. In religious art, there are innumerable depictions of angelic beings. In fact, inscribed in the glorious interior of the great Cathedral Basilica of Saint Louis the King (Saint Louis, Missouri), which has over 83,000 square feet of Byzantine and Romanesque (Italian) mosaic works by different artists, the angels are the most prominent artistic element.

## *Christian Mysticism*

The narrative sections of this book are the result of seeking true illumination. Each section includes poetry to elevate and poetically illustrate the purposeful actions of the angelic brothers. Through our contemplation and meditation, our *ascesis* (Latin, "asceticism"), the ancient mystical tradition of the Church continues. Throughout history, much angelic knowledge was obtained via mysticism and mystical encounters by advanced disciples. Similar to traditions *extra Christianum*, the Christian mystical tradition was written about, practiced, and carried from the early Church through the Middle Ages by an inexhaustible number of saints, some known and others nameless. The Desert Fathers and Mothers of the Church developed the inner prayer of silence, the prayer of quiet, and the Jesus prayer formula that grew into the Hesychasm Doctrine of the Orthodox Church in 1351. It flourished on the holy island of Mount Athos and other monastic communities. In a unique blend with the Druidic nature religion, the golden age of Celtic Christianity and mysticism flourished ca. 400-900 A.D. During the 12th century, the Anglo-Norman invasion and the Gregorian Reform installed the Roman Catholic diocesan model over Celtic Christian monasteries. Worthy of note, a majority of religions throughout world antiquity defined their foundational theology upon a trinity. These three substantial deities Carl Jung expounded upon as an archetype of humanity.

Although the politics of the Reformation and the eventual political revolutions and Inquisitions setup throughout Europe negatively impacted the formal teaching of mysticism and the Church in general, the tradition was carried into the 1500s by Western saints such as Teresa of Avila and John of the Cross, OCD. Alternatively, the Eastern Church's mysticism prevailed under political sieges throughout the Medieval and Renaissance periods. The tradition extended profoundly into the 1600s by the holy, mystical life of Maria of Agreda, OIC among others, during the great Spanish and European Renaissance. Thomas Merton, the Trappist monk and mystic teacher of the 1950s and '60s, brought to light the fact that one need not search afar, but deeply, for the mystical truth within Christianity woven through the fabric of Church history, in the teachings, scriptures, and writings of its educators and saints. Moreover, personal spiritual experience is quite valuable in confirming truth, in conjunction with devotion and study.

Although passages in each of the main topics of this book are duly referenced, there is also a mystical avenue which adds to the growing knowledge of the angelic kingdom. In summary, the essence of this book is not intended to be an exhaustive philosophical treatment of angelology or the angelic kingdom. Nor is the intention to delineate every miniscule duty the angels perform. That knowledge has already been treated in philosophical discourses, esoteric literature, and is appropriate for a foundation. The intention here is to convey direct revelational experience, as much as is allowed by our heavenly brothers and the author's limitations. Christianity contains both asceticism and corporal acts of mercy in its salvation plan. These are internal and external complementary paths. Does not Christianity found it's Old Testament theology on the Law (external obedience to divine law) and the Prophets (mystical, internal obedience to divine law)? One's religion should naturally over time bring one to the interior gates of the inward path. As this develops in the aspirant and disciple, the extraordinary outer experiences will make more sense because of the inner revelational reality. The inward path is one of self-knowledge and at the same time divine knowledge, because the approach to the soul inwardly entwines with the Holy Spirit seated in the soul.

## *A Brief History*

The ancient Jews did not start naming angels until after the Babylonian Captivity ended in 538 B.C., a grant of King Cyrus the Great. The intricate angelology of the Babylonians via Zoroastrianism influenced them by their return to Jerusalem. Moving into the Christian era, Clement of Alexandria (c. A.D. 215), an early Church Father, wrote about a cosmic hierarchy featuring the divine order of the Divine Face, the Seven Beings first created, the Archangels, and the Angels. He further showered light on a process of initiation, i.e., spiritual growth and expansion that ascends a cosmic ladder. This entails growth and eventual alchemy of humans into angels, of angels into archangels, and of archangels into *Protocists*, higher beings who then can mentor the archangels. Origen, of the same period, also had a rendition of the Celestial Hierarchy which featured knowledge of the celestial hierarchy as delineated by Saint Paul. This was knowledge handed down to the second generation of the Apostolic Fathers after the students of the Apostles themselves. In the 5th Century, a monk named Dionysius the Areopagite (a pen name), wrote a corpus of works that included defining the angelic hierarchy in three tiers of celestial ranks. Saint Thomas Aquinas (A.D. 1274) followed suit in affirming these celestial ranks and their purposes through a rigorous philosophical discourse. Pope Saint Gregory the Great (A.D. 614) wrote of the angelic hierarchy. St. Gregory's ordering differed somewhat from Dionysius and Aquinas, but the roles remained the same.

Indeed, Saint Paul the Apostle, a "Pharisee's Pharisee" and the great Christian mystical teacher and orator, influenced the lineage of spiritual teaching on the subject. Therefore, Christian Angelology, the formal study of angels, was born in the Old Testament (and before that in cultures older than Judaism) but was continued through Saint Paul. No doubt he inherited knowledge from mystical Judaism and by way of mystical experience or divine revelation, as recorded in his writings. His authority effuses it. Those who followed him made contributions to angelology, to include, *but are not limited to*: Hierotheos the Thesmothete, Saint Dionysius/Denys; Philo, Clement, and Origen of Alexandria; Tertullian of Carthage;

Augustine of Hippo; Dionysius the Areopagite; Saint Gregory the Great; Hugh and Richard of Saint Victor; Saint Thomas Aquinas; Saint Bonaventure; and John Duns Scotus, OFM.

Many ancient manuscripts talk about the angels. Some ancient texts like The Celestial Hierarchy by Dionysius the Areopagite, Saint Paul's letters, the Book of Revelation in the New Testament, and The Book of Enoch, the latter of which was very commonly read in the Early Church, describe at length the angelic kingdom. The Ante-Nicene Fathers, the Apostolic Fathers who lived between the first generation after the Apostles until the First Council of Nicaea in A.D. 325, also wrote about the angels, their orders, and hierarchy.

> "The Jews and the early Fathers of the Church divided the heavens into circles or zones, each inhabited by its peculiar powers or intelligent natures, differing in dignity and in might. The central place was assigned to God Himself, and to Christ, who sat on His right hand, and who is called by the Fathers of the Church the 'Angel of the Church,' and the 'Angel of the New Covenant.' Next in order came 'Thrones,' 'Archangels,' 'Cherubim and Seraphim,' and most remote from God's throne the 'Chorus of Angels,' the *tutelar genii* (personal deific protectors) of men. The system of zones and powers seems to have been derived from the Chaldeans, who made a similar division of the heavens. According to this idea, Arnobius speaks of Christ as nearest to the Father, and God of the 'inner powers,' who enjoyed God's immediate presence."[2]

The Book of Enoch, apocryphal in the Roman Church, was included in the Ethiopian Canon of scripture and was also uncovered in the Dead Sea Scrolls at Qumran. The scrolls are an extant collection of sacred writings of the Essene community in the Judean desert before, during, and after the birth of Jesus. It contains angelic knowledge, including prophetic references to the coming of Christ. The Epistle of Jude in the New Testament directly quotes the Book of Enoch.

"Irenaeus and Clement of Alexandria cited the *Book of Enoch* without questioning its sacred character. Thus, Irenaeus, assigning to the *Book of Enoch* an authenticity analogous to that of

[2] Philip Schaff, *The Ante-Nicene Fathers, The Seven Books of Arnobius Against the Heathen*, translated by Hamilton Bryce and Hugh Campbell, Christian Classics Ethereal Library, Grand Rapids, http://www.ccel.org/ccel/schaff/anf10.html, Accessed 16 February 2025.

Mosaic literature, affirms that Enoch, although a man, filled the office of God's messenger to the Angels. Tertullian adds, "But as Enoch has spoken in the same scripture of the Lord (the Epistle of Jude), and 'every scripture suitable for edification is divinely inspired,' let us reject nothing which belongs to us. It may now seem to have been disavowed by the Jews like all other scripture which speaks of Christ. Tertullian confirms (these views) by appealing to the testimony of the Apostle Jude. Origen, in quoting Hebrew literature, assigns to the Book of Enoch the same authority as the Psalms."[3]

"The Book of Enoch was once cherished by Jews and Christians alike, but this book later fell into disfavor with powerful theologians precisely because of its controversial statements on the nature and deeds of the fallen angels. There is abundant proof that Christ approved of the Book of Enoch. Over a hundred phrases in the New Testament find precedents in the Book of Enoch. Another remarkable bit of evidence for the early Christians' acceptance of the Book of Enoch was for many years buried under the King James Bible's mistranslation of Luke 9:35, describing the transfiguration of Christ: 'And there came a voice out of the cloud, saying, This is my beloved Son: hear him.' Apparently, the translator here wished to make this verse agree with a similar verse in Matthew and Mark. But Luke's verse in the original Greek reads: 'This is my Son, the Elect One [from the Greek *ho eklelegmenos*, lit., 'the elect one']: hear him.' 'The Elect One' is a most significant term (found fourteen times) in the Book of Enoch. If the book was indeed known to the apostles of Christ, with its abundant descriptions of the Elect One who should 'sit upon the throne of glory' and the Elect One who should 'dwell in the midst of them,' then the great scriptural authenticity is accorded to the Book of Enoch when the 'voice out of the cloud' tells the apostles, 'This is my Son, the Elect One'— the one promised in the Book of Enoch."[4]

And finally, the Book of Enoch is included in the canon of the Ethiopian Orthodox Tewahedo, the Eritrean Orthodox Tewahedo Churches, and the Ethiopian Jewish community Beta Israel. Enoch is mentioned four (4) times in the Christian Bible, as one who walked with and pleased God.

[3] *The Book of Enoch the Prophet*, translated by Richard Laurence (London: Kegan Paul, Trench & Co., 1883).
[4] *The Complete Book of Enoch, Standard English Version*, translated by Dr. Jay Winter (Winter Publications, 2015).

*Subhuman and Superhuman Angels*

The Celestial Hierarchy established by Church theologians that follows later under the section heading of Book Framework, includes the "superhuman angels", but neither includes the subhuman angelic strata, nor the strata of the "left-hand path", the demons and black magicians. As much as the Celestial Powers who reside in the angelic kingdom have worked to attain their position in the army of God, so too, have the demons earned their place, through their own desires and actions, in the netherworld in rebellion to the holiness of God. Another point of delineation regards the subhuman stage, i.e., the level where angelic spirits are not self-conscious. These spirits are called elementals and lesser angels for the purposes of this treatment. Elementals and lesser angels overlap as the builders of nature up and through the higher planes. The lesser angels characterize the realms of the unseen natural world, and are popularly known as sylphs, faeries, gnomes, elves, etc. In their hordes and myriads these beings, great and small, with a number of other subtler classifications, attend to the cycles of seasons, weather, and the plant, mineral, and animal kingdoms of our world. They are guided by greater angelic beings and advanced saints. Still others not relegated to these lower etheric-physical plane orders populate other departments of higher planes, beyond the physical plane, mostly unknown to us, expanding to the higher planetary and cosmic architecture outside this planet.

Suffice to say, certain orders of angels attend to and communicate with humanity. Three such examples among numerous possible citations from the Bible, read:

> "For he commands his angels with regard to you, to guard you wherever you go." (Psalm 91:11)

> "See that you do not despise one of these little ones, for I say to you that their angels in heaven always look upon the face of my heavenly Father." (Matthew 18:10)

> "Now, go…where I have told you. See, my angel will go before you." (Exodus 32:34)

Overall, then, the Angelic Kingdom attends to ALL evolutionary life processes of this planet. A quick citing of such duties can be found in Revelation 7:1, 14:18, and 16:5. They are the invisible builders and workers, ultimately directed by God, Whose blueprint for Creation they fulfill. There has been, and will continue to be, a broad veil between the communication of human and most angelic ranks. This is not a hard and fast rule, as much as we humans like to make hard and fast rules. Our guardian angels and the archangels are frequent exceptions, as they are most often encountered attending humanity. Exceptions in the Bible include the times when even the great superhuman Archangelic Lords (*The Seven Spirits Who Stand before the Throne*) were witnessed by Saint John the Apostle in the Book of Revelation, as well as in other passages in Revelation depicting the greater angelic beings. Isaiah the prophet also had a similar encounter at the court of The Almighty with the Seraphim. Communication of divine wisdom from angels is divinely blessed (allowed) when the soul in incarnation, on this physical plane, is aligned with God's will. They are so pure that it can only be this way.

> "Because into a soul that plots evil, wisdom does not enter,
>
> nor does she dwell in a body under debt of sin." (Wisdom 1:4)

The angels who communicate with humanity do so to aid us in our strivings to do good or to impart knowledge in the minor Christian Mysteries. But there is no bargaining of credit for promised future good behavior. Certain groups of angels are always aiding humanity in the background, remaining unseen and unknown.

This veil is of necessity to ensure a safer world from the human standpoint. A divine benediction. The angelic kingdom, composed of vast armies of spirit-beings far outnumbering the human race, ranges from subhuman to superhuman, and the subhuman are in large part on a separate evolutionary arc from humanity. Nothing in Cosmos is static, and just as the spirit of Man utilized the physical vehicle of early animal-man of nascent mind, so too the angels evolve in consciousness through lower grade incorporeal bodies to higher grade "spiritual bodies."

> The first man, Adam, became a living being,
>
> the last Adam a life-giving spirit.
>
> But the spiritual was not first;

rather the natural and then the spiritual.

The first man was from the earth, earthly;

the second man, from heaven.

As was the earthly one, so also are the earthly,

and as is the heavenly one, so also are the heavenly.

Just as we have borne the image of the earthly one,

we shall also bear the image of the heavenly one. (1 Corinthians 15:45-49)

Thus, we are two separate hierarchies advancing together. The superhuman angels progressed ages ago through that subhuman stage of involution and are now God-conscious to one degree or another. They are more spiritually advanced than most of humanity. This will not always be so, but for now it is the state of the union. They are more ancient than humanity. How do we know that? Recall in the *Book of Job*, when the Lord God asked Job:

Where were you when I founded the earth?

… and who laid its cornerstone,

While the morning stars sang together

and all the sons of God shouted for joy? (Job 38:4-7)

The "sons of God" at that point in time did not include humans, but the angels, who were here from the foundations of the world, veritably as the builders of the Logos's Creation through the Cosmic Christ.

### *The Book of Life*

Lesser angels and elementals respond and grow along the lines of color and sound. They see sound and hear color, the opposite of human growth. Sound is a form in the invisible world, as any scientific book on music will show that musical notes create a form. This is why angels create symbols oftentimes on the inner planes to communicate. Each sound also has an associated color. One can follow, then, that when these colors and sounds are coordinated through rhythmic incantation or formula, the subhuman angelic forces can be directed, subject to anyone who has the knowledge. These formulas, as a matter of record, are kept in "The Book of Life," a book mentioned a number of times in the Bible, with a few citations listed below:

I saw the dead, the great and the lowly, standing before the throne, and scrolls were opened. Then another scroll was opened, the Book of Life. The dead were judged according to their deeds, by what was written in the scrolls. (Revelation 20:12)

May they be blotted from the Book of Life; not registered among the just! (Psalm 69:29)

Yes, and I ask you also, my true yokemate, to help them, for they have struggled at my side in promoting the gospel, along with Clement and my other co-workers, whose names are in *the Book of Life* (Philippians 4:3)

…but nothing unclean will enter it, nor any[one] who does abominable things or tells lies. Only those will enter whose names are written in the Lamb's Book of Life. (Revelation 21:27)

*The Book* is also referred to as the *Akashic Record* in esoteric parlance, which certain angels meticulously keep. They are kept high on "heavenly" planes, on "scrolls of light". This is not the same as the "astral light," which records the impressions on the astral plane. The Akashic Record, or Book of Life, is the true record. Whereas the planes of heaven are like a spiritual ladder of greater and lesser consciousness in the invisible part of the creation of God, recall that the Master Jesus also said, "In my Father's house there are many dwelling places." (John 14:2) According to divine plan and purpose, then, the divine formulas contained in the Book of Life can be directed toward the lesser angels/elementals in sounds and colors, combined with words, signs, and objects of power, which elicit their response, automatic in nature.

To illustrate, let us review the tactics of Joshua to conquer the walled city of Jericho.

"And to Joshua the Lord said: I have delivered Jericho, its king, and its warriors into your power. Have all the soldiers circle the city, marching once around it. Do this for six days, with seven priests carrying rams' horns ahead of the ark (the Ark of the Covenant). On the seventh day march around the city seven times, and have the priests blow the horns. When they give a long blast on the rams' horns and you hear the sound of the horn, all the people shall shout aloud. The wall of the city will collapse, and the people shall attack straight ahead." (Joshua 6:2-5)


In this example from the Old Testament, Joshua the son of Nun, a close associate and trusted general of Moses, followed the Lord's instructions, a formula for control of the nature angels, and the Wall of Jericho collapsed. He directed the angels who uphold the matter aspect of nature, who are not self-conscious at this stage. It becomes obvious what this knowledge in the wrong hands could do. There are other reasons why humans are separated from the angelic kingdom, as a rule. Humans, although brothers to the angels, yet hardly conscious of it in the main, do not have the advanced wisdom/knowledge and do not have the same path of spiritual growth.  Complications arise in the conflict of human and angelic goals for growth, which could be dangerous to humans when personal contact is made in the wrong way, especially with an angel of the subhuman species. Human growth is oriented toward love and its power of connecting or bringing together. Angelic growth is oriented toward intelligence, which demonstrates in activity in matter. In other words, angels advance in growth toward the Creator through feeling which they get from the vibration (activity) of matter. Hence, their sensitivities elevate higher and higher to the vibration of all things in their divine mystery. It is safest when angels are encountered on the high mental or soul plane in the Holy of Holies of meditation, but it is not safe down here on Earth in the lower mental, astral/emotional, and physical planes of our everyday lives. I elaborate more about having a relationship with the angelic brothers in the latter part of the book in the chapter on "The Angels."

The secret formulas that are kept in the Book of Life, that direct the subhuman angelic multitudes, are known to The Christ and the advanced Saints of our race (East and West) because they have become selfless in wisdom and love. They have conquered all the illusions of this world—all that is transient in this world. As St. Paul states, "For the things that are seen are transient, but the things that are unseen are eternal." (2 Corinthians 4:18) Humanity disrupts the lesser angels and elementals in their divine work when humanity violates the sacred laws of Nature. Bombs and wars, as an example, send the lower angelic forces into a boomerang of chaos that rebounds eventually onto the human race through environmental calamities. For every action there is a reaction. They need our help and cooperation to create the intended paradise on this planet for the Plan of God.

The angels' collective wisdom draws from the vastness of God's wisdom of the Cosmos, the manifested Creation. The secrets of that wisdom are only given to humanity when the race is ready for it. Each order of the Celestial Powers has apportioned access to it. And for clarification, the Akashic Record or The Book of Life is not a volume of wisdom, but that of records. The Book, of what has occurred and has been recorded on the mental plane matter (spiritual light) is kept sacredly, secretly, and securely by the angels.

<u>*Book Framework*</u>

The following outline amalgamates from the aforesaid teachers, the angelic hierarchy in Christian mystical terms, which is principally derived from the Old and New Testament:

- The Seven Spirits Who Stand before the Throne
- 1$^{st}$ Triad; Seraphim, Cherubim, and Thrones
- 2$^{nd}$ Triad; Dominions (Dominations), Powers, and Virtues
- 3$^{rd}$ Triad; Princedoms (Principalities), Archangels, and Angels

As shown above, *The Seven Spirits Who Stand before the Throne* are great Archangelic Lords who receive the Divine Ray of God through the Holy Trinity and flow God's distinct spiritual energies through their army of angelic beings below them. So there are in actuality seven armies, each one ruled by one of the Seven Spirits to build and maintain the plan of God. This is the great unity of God's sublime spiritual differentiation into "all that is visible and invisible." To this point, there are also many subdivisions in each order of the hierarchy. An analogy can be made to the human kingdom. In the field of law, there is a Supreme Court of the land, and many subsidiary courts corresponding to localities. Assigned to the courts there are: Judicial Law Clerks; Lawyers; Arbitrators, Mediators, and Conciliators; Administrative Law Judges, Adjudicators, and Hearing Officers, etc., Judges, Abstractors, and Searchers. So even though there are seemingly 10 streamlined orders of the angelic hierarchy, there is a complex substrata mostly unknown to, or unrecognized by, general humanity.

<u>*First Contact with Angels*</u>

I knew nothing about angels and was unaware of the spiritual world as a young man growing up. Although as a child I could see the energies and their movements on the etheric planes, the next level of matter up from the physical gaseous state, I quickly learned to keep silent about it, hiding it from friends, teachers and parents. As a young man, my introduction to the angelic world came abruptly. At the age of twenty-four, I was playing basketball in the English Basketball League in Nottingham, England after completing college at Loyola Maryland. A few months into the season, horrific nightmares would take hold of me in my sleep. I felt as if I was being strangled and seized by an evil force. I would be deathly afraid upon waking, because I could not get rid of the terrors and had no spiritual foundation by which to understand it. I met a man named Ken through my mentor and second mother, Joyce, a teammate's parent. Ken was a mystic, and he offered to help. After talking to him to try to make sense out of what was happening, I went to sleep that night hoping that something would change for the better. When the same terrifying event was about to happen during sleep, I awoke springing upright in a sweat to a "white wind" swirling around me. This spiritual, energetic whirlwind was extracting a number of black demons into the whipping breath of its turbulence. After blinking and rubbing my eyes clear in those incredulous moments, I looked into what I now know as the astral plane and saw a white winged angel flying past my face into a bright light at the far end of the room (the light did not exist in the physical room). No words were spoken to me. The angel selflessly helped me by extricating the demons, then flew away. I am grateful to this day for the help I received from these two friends and the holy angel in such an ordeal.

This event was the opening to the spiritual world for me. I knew I had to figure out all that had happened to me, and more; but first I had to shelve it for a few years to deal with other things young men have to figure out in life to make their way. Faith, religion, and spirituality became a lifelong pursuit as I turned twenty-six and entered the US Air Force. There can be similar turning points in anyone's life. For me, I realized that the external culture of our world is not all that it appears to be (illusory), and that alignment with my soul's purpose in life should be the crux of the external expression. This is something that can get buried by the over-emphasis of and immersion in the dominant culture, sometimes referred to as the "over-culture or secular world." And my first experience with an "angel ally" was important to recognize. The spiritual, mystical avenue opened up to me gradually as I dedicated and disciplined myself to conform to spiritual practices aimed at walking closer with God. This book, in part, is an expression of that journey. It's a journey any person can access in the inner light with the soul.

*The Writing of this Book*

Prayer, investigation, and examination (devotion and science) prepared this book with hope to encourage men and women in the pursuit of union with our divine source, God. Yet, at the commencement of entertaining the idea of this book, I hesitated and complained, like Jonah, of the magnitude of this undertaking. I felt that I could not possibly shoulder the task. And surely, I proposed, so many doctors of letters were better qualified. But in longing for wisdom and truth, I researched numerous books, modern, apocryphal, and arcane. This seemed to be my assignment of more spiritual homework for edification in holiness. I kept a journal of spiritual dreams and contemplative visions that carried messages from angels along the way.

I began pointed research on what has been written about the angelic hierarchy in 2023. The intent was to write a book from the annals of Christian traditions to shine light on the wisdom and beauty of the angels within the Christian context. In March of that year, in meditation I was encouraged to concentrate hard as I began to feel spiritual energy fill my head. This is always a grace. I then saw a gold key fit into a lock which freed open a door. I shut the door behind me after entering. Winged angels (not all angels are winged) appeared in the room, which was filled with a cloud of light. Beautiful spirits with wondrous wings stirred the air above me.  Words cannot describe the purity and beauty of that environ around me. Out in front, I saw the greater landscape of a canyon of shimmering white marble buildings upon rocky mountains. I was then lifted by my angelic brothers and carried to a higher promontory for a greater view. I lost consciousness for a while. When I came to, I was told that my angelic brothers would always be with me as long as I lived a harmless holy life. As I was resolved to live the life of a celibate monk, they confided that loving a woman would be good too, which opens the heart. They also said that I would see things here, in this place, of which I have only dreamed. The gate to the angelic hierarchy opens to a place of harmlessness and to a portion of the Divine Mind and Will of God the Creator.

Even so, I was quite unaware of what was about to happen as the research period neared its end.

In April 2024, I heard a sharp voice while lying awake on my bed, which said, "Pay attention!" I was alone in the house. I shut my eyes to concentrate and fell into a vision experience with Mother Mary, the Blessed Virgin, Who said she wanted me to witness with my life my union with Her. As St Paul once stated, I didn't know whether I was in the spiritual body or out of it.

I rose up to pray once I realized what just happened, moving across the room to my habitual place of prayer. As prayers flowed into deeper contemplation, a door appeared, and a light turned on behind it. With faith I entered through it. From there I was summoned to another hall where multiple doors faced me. I was told to open the third door, a room with light flooding through the windows. Further inside, a spirit angel told me to wait for Mother Mary. Soon a woman entered the inner room with a gold crown on her head and a diaphanous white veil that flowed to the ground. It was my Holy Mother. I bowed as she sat on an elevated chair a few steps opposite me. She told me to approach. I did and knelt in front of her. She also told me to straighten up, that I was a son of God. After giving me some instructions about using mental discipline in navigating the interior planes, She, knowing that I was confounded as to how to reach the angelic spirits, said, "You will represent Me to the angels. You are now in the Hall of Wisdom." I was then given a vision of a Great Pyramid on the higher mental planes and a view of where the Hall of Wisdom is located in that ethereal space.

I asked, "How will I find the angels?"

My Holy Mother explained, "Enter into the Light (the inner Holy of Holies where one is protected) during meditation and They will find you. You will gain the knowledge of the Ancient Brotherhood held secret and sacred for only those who are ready to receive it. Accept it in humility. And likewise distribute it in humility. Your book will be profound and set the minds of many to wonder of the wealth of God's coffers, awaiting all who strive and persevere and attain."

Days later, in contemplative prayer, an angel approached me. He said he was sent to me from holy Michael the Archangel. He said he would teach me of the angelic kingdom and proceeded to show me the Book of Life. He told me I must write of the angelic wonders that are written in the Book.

Me: "But I am nobody. I am unholy."

Angel: "You have been chosen and accepted to write of the wonders of which men can't dream."

Me: "Then take me wherever you will."

I am oft reminded, for good reason, about the divine grace required to learn from and have access to the holy angels. In addition, I have need, like any Christian on the path, for the use of right speech which raises one's sanctity. Why? Because it is what proceeds from one's mouth that defiles a soul. Therein, I recommitted my life to God, to strive to do good, albeit as an imperfect servant. I refer the reader back to the very first line of this introduction for Saint Paul's sage words.

*Illustrations*

Unless otherwise annotated, paintings with no credit in the footnotes are by the author under inspiration of the Holy Spirit. Other depictions are classical paintings in the public domain. These painted forms representing the Celestial Powers are merely a device of art and do not accurately depict the divine spirits themselves. The angels are formless in that they occupy a higher plane than the gross physical plane of dense matter of which human bodies consist. Their atoms vibrate at a higher rate. They can change that vibration (slow it down) in order to appear to human sight. They have and do often appear as human in a form congenial to the expectations of the human viewer. Why? …so that They won't scare us to death!

Withal, I am very grateful to the Most High God, great in mercy, and for the immense sacrifices of our holy ones, the saints who have mastered this physical plane, who sacrificially and compassionately remain here attached to Earth to teach and guide us on the road they themselves have trod. I am grateful for the angelic hierarchy, because the only way this book would be completed would be by their gift of knowledge. Am also grateful for the graces and ineffable patience of Master Jesus and Blessed Mother Mary, Who deign to inspire me with this work, and without Whom this book would not be possible.

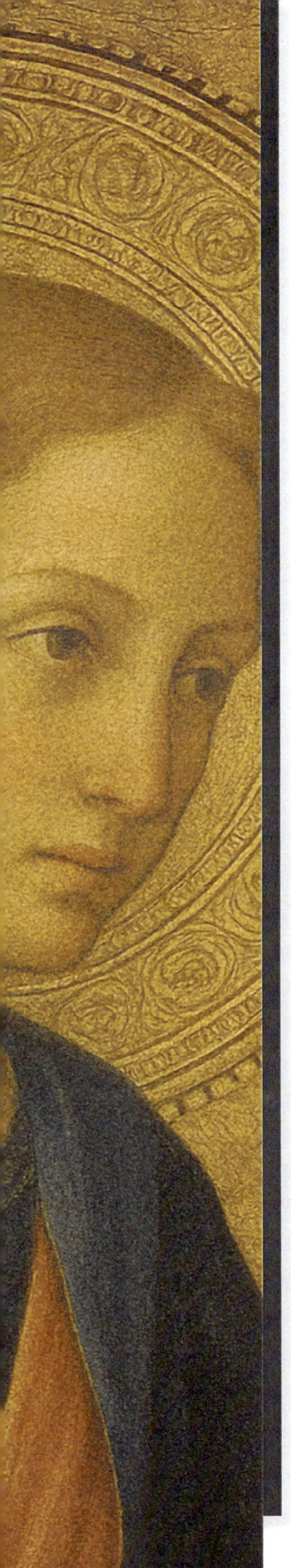



*"John, to the seven churches in Asia: Grace to you and peace from
him who is and who was and who is to come, and from the seven
spirits before his throne, and from Jesus Christ, the faithful witness,
the firstborn of the dead and ruler of the kings of the earth. To him
who loves us and has freed us from our sins by his blood, who has
made us into a kingdom, priests for his God and
Father, to him be glory and power forever [and ever]."*
(Revelation 1:4-6)

*"Seven flaming torches burned in front of the throne,
which are the seven spirits of God."*
(Revelation 4:5)

The Being of the unmanifested God, the Logos, in order to project into Cosmos or Creation, differentiates as a trinity of Father, Son, and Holy Spirit. For our Eastern brothers it would be as Shiva, Vishnu, Brahma. Still further God divides the one dominant ray of his essence into seven cosmic rays or fires, a septenary, through the *Seven Spirits Who Stand before the Throne*. These seven Archangelic Lords distribute the Logos' seven distinct energies throughout the world through the hosts of the angelic hierarchy of spirits aligned with them. As Dionysius writes, the divine rays of the Logos outpour to the highest beings, and then to all in manifestation. As an analogy, there is one white light, and from it three prime colors (a trinity, if you will), and then seven basic colors differentiate further. Likewise, the *Seven Spirits Who Stand before the Throne*, or Archangelic Lords, flow divine energy received from the one Logos to build their part of God's plan. In Judaism they are known as the Elohim. In Sikhism, Hinduism, and Theosophy, they are known as the Seven Rishis.

*The Seven Spirits Who Stand before the Throne* can be understood in their animated attributes in human terms as the energetic, celestial rays of: (1) Will, (2) Love blended with Wisdom, (3) Intelligence-infused Matter, (4) Harmony of Beauty, (5) Rational Science, (6) Single-Pointed Devotion of Idealism, and (7) Divine Ritual. All these attributes are not distributed by flooding them into the world but are levied in measured paces by the seven Archangelic Lords according to the divine plan of God. Some are even withdrawn completely for a phase depending on the evolutionary circumstances of the planet and the needs of our human, animal, plant, and mineral kingdoms. Thus the evolutionary seasons of the divine plan dictate the amounts and intensities of each "sub-ray" of the Logos. This flow can be observed and validated not just in the macrocosm of the planet, but also reflects in the human anatomy and mental/emotional makeup over the span of a lifetime.

The sense of the whole in this knowledge is that the angelic kingdom links our entire life-sphere between human, angel, and the natural world, seen and unseen, of this planet and the greater Cosmos. The interrelated hierarchies truly show that the entirety of this world is connected and is One, and that the spiritual (human) and angelic hierarchies are interdependent.

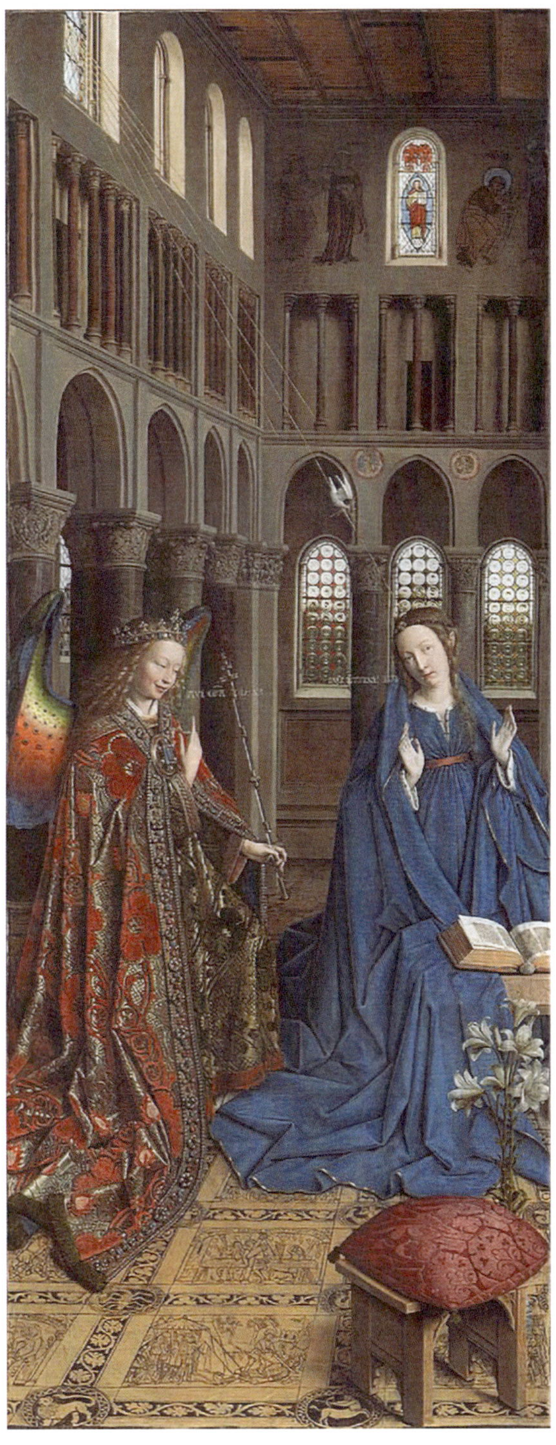

[5] Jan van Eyck, *The Annunciation*, c. 1434/1436, Andrew W. Mellon Collection, The National Gallery of Art, Washington, D.C. *Courtesy National Gallery of Art, Washington, DC.*

IN AN ELEGANT PORTRAYAL of the truth of *The Seven Spirits Who Stand before the Throne* of God, one can see the seven rays of light shining down through an upper stained-glass window onto the Blessed Virgin Mary in *The Annunciation* by Jan Van Eyck (1434). Next to Her, the Archangel Gabriel is depicted with rainbow-arrayed wings

# SONNET TO THE SEVEN SPIRITS WHO STAND BEFORE THE THRONE

Beyond the mountaintops from sacred isle

The Trinity will strew the perfect seed

To fructify the seven groves that need

Intelligence and Mother-matter's smile

Whose Beauty is a path the angels tile

Their flooded fields have grown what God decreed

That every son of man, should they succeed

Has hewn the ladder of a life of trial

Let concrete science scour temple halls

Revealing splendor rightfully insane

And pour Devotion drunk within its walls

With Ritual whose priest unveils the plain

Its Power clears our eyes like waterfalls

The thunder of the archangelic thane

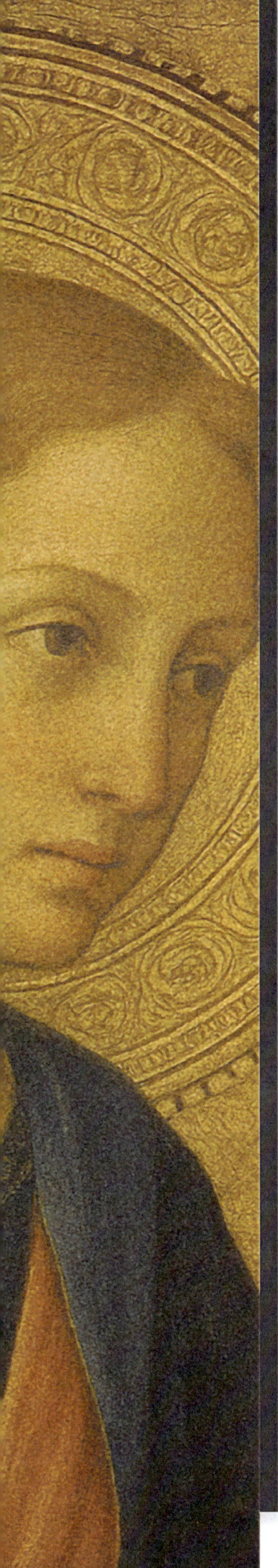



"The name 'Seraphim' does not come from charity only, but from the excess of charity, expressed by the word… 'fire.' Hence Dionysius (Coel. Hier. vii) expounds the name 'Seraphim' according to the properties of fire, containing an excess of heat. Now in fire we may consider three things. First, the movement which is upwards and continuous. This signifies that they are borne inflexibly towards God. Secondly, the active force which is 'heat,' which is not found in fire simply, but exists with a certain sharpness, as being of most penetrating action, and reaching even to the smallest things, and, as it were, with superabundant fervor; whereby is signified the action of these angels, exercised powerfully upon those who are subject to them, rousing them to a like fervor, and cleansing them wholly by their heat. Thirdly we consider in fire the quality of clarity, or brightness, which signifies that these angels have in themselves an inextinguishable light, and that they also perfectly enlighten others."[6]

"The name Seraphim clearly indicates their ceaseless and eternal revolution about Divine Principles, their heat and keenness, the exuberance of their intense, perpetual, tireless activity, and their elevative and energetic assimilation of those below, kindling them and firing them to their own heat, and wholly purifying them by a burning and all-consuming flame; and by the unhidden, unquenchable, changeless, radiant and enlightening power, dispelling and destroying the shadows of darkness."[7]

Spiritual fire has other forms that affect humans. Fire is another term for "energy" and "light" in a mystical sense. Physical "fire by friction" we normally

[6] Thomas Aquinas, *The Summa Theologica, Article 108*, translated by Fathers of the English Dominican Province (Burns, Oates & Washbourne Ltd., London, 1920).
[7] Dionysius the Areopagite, *The Celestial Hierarchy*, www.ccel.org, Christian Classics Ethereal Library, Grand Rapids, accessed 12/19/2024.

see and detect with the senses as it provides heat and light. And, invisible to human eyes, other spiritual fires affect the soul and spirit of a human being. Anytime someone's "light shines," they are transmitting their soul's "fire" to those around them. Let not thy light be hid beneath the bushel basket!

There are a number of other cosmic fires or divine energies of God that perform other work in Creation at the hands of the angels. Through the angelic kingdom is transmitted "wholly intelligible Light" (Dionysius). Seraphim are the first transmitters after God, Who after the being of The Holy Trinity is further embodied at the next lower level by *The Seven Spirits Who Stand before the Throne*. Entire books are written on these subjects of divine energies. However, it merits saying that the angelic kingdom serves as a vehicle of employing constructive and destructive energies throughout our world. The human race is important in this dynamic too, not least of which because we are under the same divine law along with the angelic kingdom. No one is excepted. The Most Holy Seraphim possess a high order of spiritual fire from their propinquity to the Godhead, and thus the divine energy in its multiple manifestations is transmitted through the Seraphim to those immediately after and below them, with clarity and purifying power. "The Seraphim are leaders to the mystical and divine contemplations…Therefore the first Order of the holy Angels possesses above all others the characteristic of fire" (Dionysius).

One can also know that the holy Seraphim make sure, at the point of discipleship, that the disciple is purified in the sight of God, whenever we sit in the divine radiance, the holy Light that emanates from God, during meditation/contemplation. This divine light raises our own contemplation higher and changes us, even at the physical and spiritual level if practiced with diligence. We see the symbology of this in the encounter Isaiah the prophet had with the Seraphim, one of whom purified him with an ember from the altar (Isaiah 6:6-7). It is also discussed in the mystical writings of The Mystical City of God by Venerable Maria of Agreda.

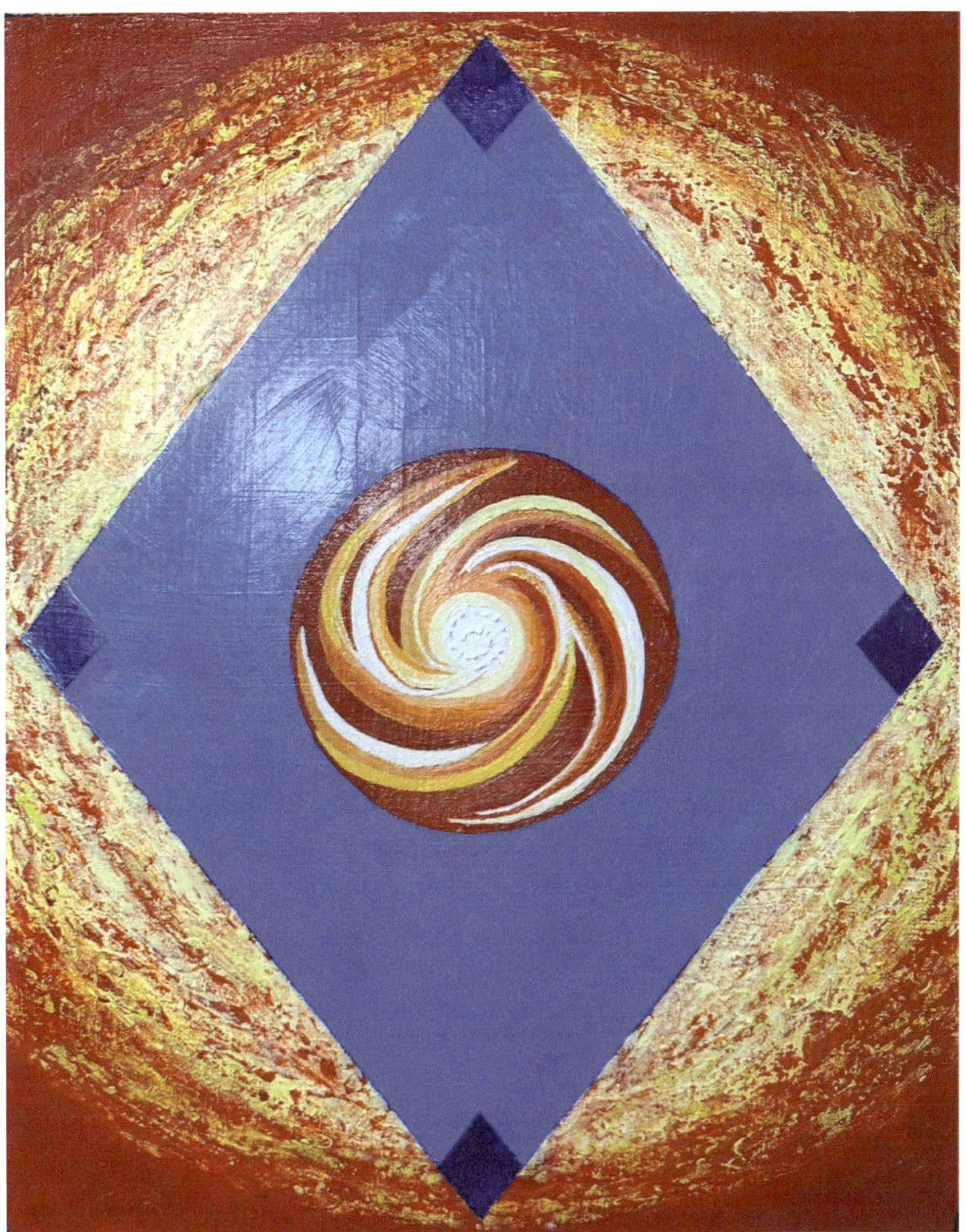

WHEN WE PEER OUT at the night sky and witness the celestial lights that array our galaxy, the Milky Way, we can gather an understanding that the physical cosmos has a foundation of Cosmic Fires. That the created universe (Intelligent Matter, the Mother, aka., the Holy Spirit) is innately ordered with incalculable precision attests to the invisible spiritual cosmic fire God uses to create the manifested systems of worlds. This is the macrocosm. It is said in the Bible and elsewhere, "God is a consuming fire." Humans as the microcosm, little images of God imprinted in the soul, also contain an invisible spiritual fire which through spiritual growth arouses and eventually enflames our being as the light within us. Light extending from us, such as in the halos of saints, is a reality for those gifted with that vision. The angels at each level in their hierarchy use types of spiritual fire to maintain and evolve Creation and aid humanity.

On 5 June 2022, in contemplation, the holy angels showed me a ball of light and how it radiated downward through the angelic planes, through and by the Seraphim filtering into the middle tier of the Dominions, Powers and Virtues, and then to the plane of the Princedoms, Archangels, and Angels. This is a process of how God's rays of wisdom and other energies diffuse and distribute downward through the angelic hierarchy. Each level or order of the sacred Celestial Powers uses what is appropriate to their level, from higher to lower.

### *The Revelation of the Light*

Certain angels have the responsibility as *Keepers of the Light* who reside in the tier of the Most Holy Seraphim. They administer the Divine Radiance, the Holy Light, experienced in the interior recesses of meditation, contemplation on the inner planes, and all levels of the angelic hierarchy. They started contacting me whilst in meditation in 2022. Not much can be made known about them.

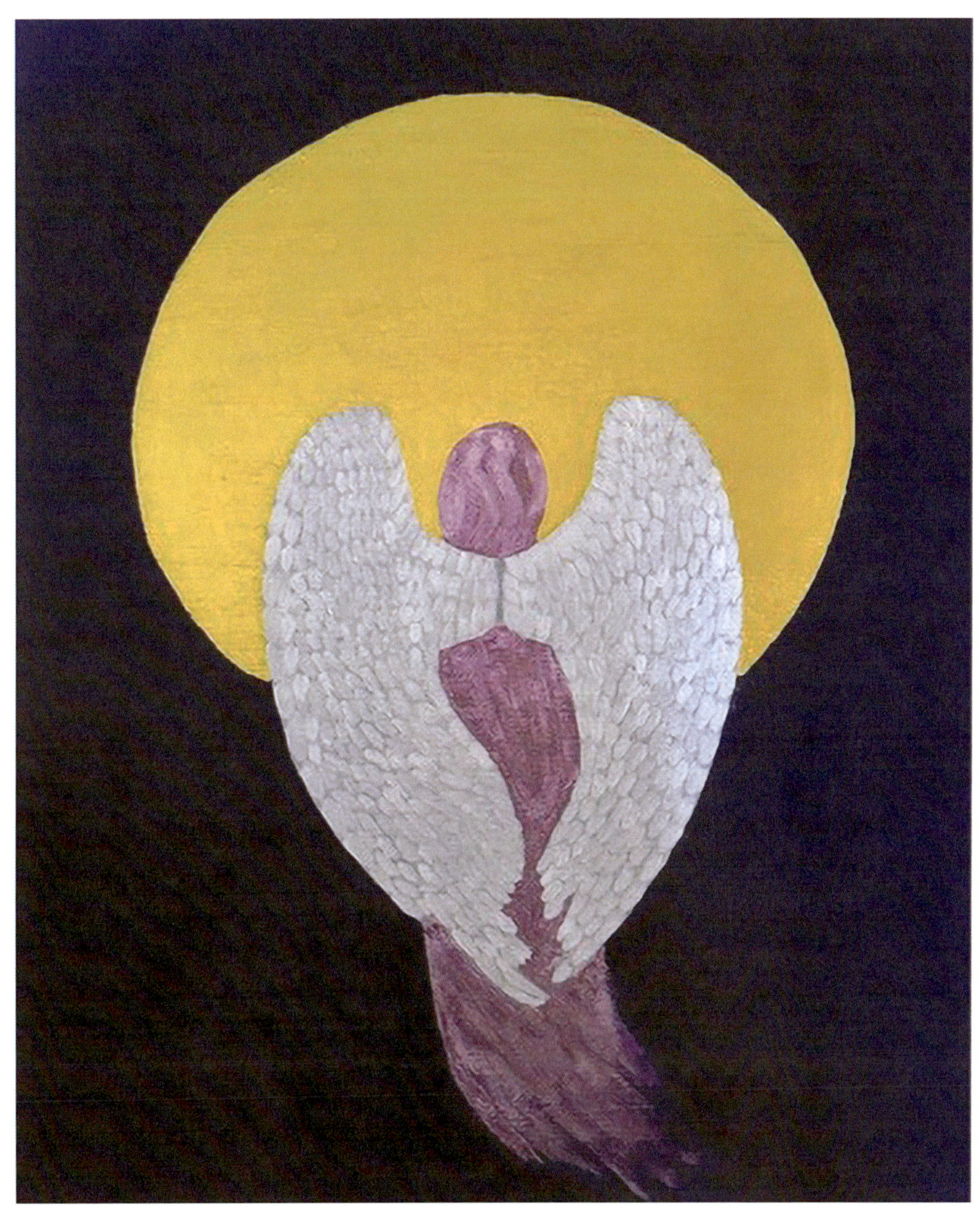

SONNET TO THE MOST HOLY SERAPHIM

The Glowing Ones create the light of day
Upon the planes that only touch the soul
The power of The Light is One and whole
And edifies angelic choirs that play
In symphony of fiery ballet
The flame of God, which lights the Golden Bowl
Attends through them its blossoming and goal
Agaze with wings that never peel away

The fires of their Light will consecrate
Devotion from a depth of love as deep
*The One Who Always Was* designed the slate
For these angelic lords who never sleep
Illuminati, Seraphim create
The sanctuaries "winds of spirit" sweep

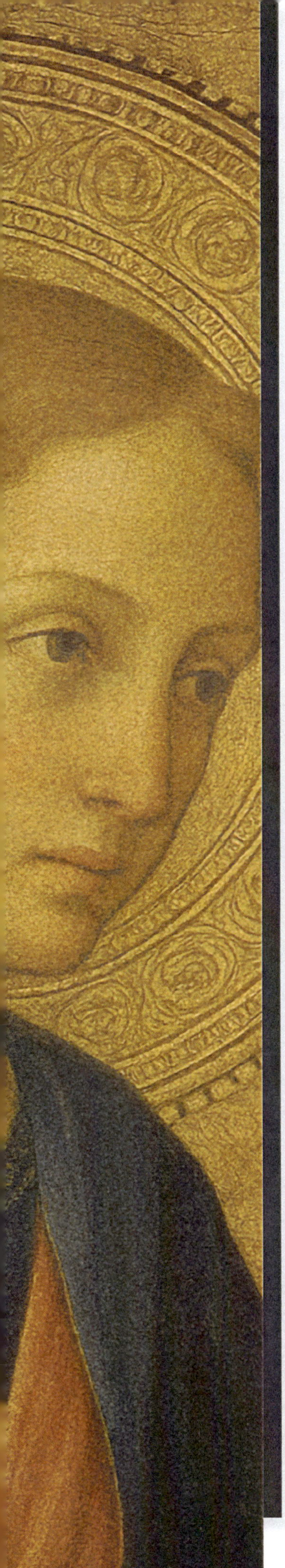

## THE CHERUBIM (STREAMS OF WISDOM)

"The name 'Cherubim' denotes their power of knowing and beholding God, their receptivity to the highest Gift of Light, their contemplation of the Beauty of the Godhead in Its First Manifestation, and that they are filled by participation in Divine Wisdom and bounteously outpour to those below them from their own fount of wisdom. We are told by Hebrew scholars that the holy name Seraphim means 'those who kindle or make hot,' (while) Cherubim denotes abundance of knowledge or an outflowing of wisdom. Reasonably, therefore, is this first Celestial Hierarchy administered by the most transcendent Natures, since it occupies a more exalted place than all the others, being immediately present with God; And because of its nearness (to God), to it are brought the first revelations and perfections of God before the rest. Therefore they are named 'The Glowing Ones' (Seraphim), 'Streams of Wisdom' (Cherubim), and 'Thrones', in illustration of their Divine Nature."[8]

"And my spirit saw the girdle which girt that house of fire and on its four sides were streams full of living fire, and they girt that house. And roundabout were Seraphim, Cherubim, and Ophannin (Thrones): And these are they who sleep not and guard the throne of His glory."[9]

In the story of Adam and Eve, God banishes the man from the Garden of Eden and stations two Cherubim to guard the way to the Tree of Life. (Genesis 3:24). This act pronounces one of the roles of the Cherubim: to watch in protection the sacred pathway which accesses the paradise of God. As we approach the Lord to search even deeper into mystical sanctity, Who is "seated upon and above the Cherubim," only holiness will allow us to proceed past the guardians of the sacred, deep into the mind of God. Here I don't mean access to God,

[8] Dionysius the Areopagite, *The Celestial Hierarchy.*
[9] *The Complete Book of Enoch.*

stamped within our souls, but the highest tier of the angelic kingdom's access to the throne or mind of the Lord of the World, the I AM. In a mystical sense, the same attitude applies to meditation. Everything we are attached to in the everyday world must be doffed, like a hat, in order to connect with the soul deep within silence.

It was divine instruction that Moses and the Israelites adhered to in constructing the Tent of Meeting to house the Ark of the Covenant. The Ark contained 1) the golden pot that had manna from the Israelites' miraculous sustenance in the desert; 2) Aaron's rod that budded, symbolizing his divinely appointed priesthood; and 3) the tablets of the covenant which among other directives had the ten commandments that Moses received from God on Mount Sinai. The Tent of Meeting was decorated with embroidery of the Cherubim. The Ark was also constructed with two Cherubim facing each other on the top cover. The Lord spoke to Moses inside the innermost room, the Holy of Holies, in the Tent of Meeting. God's voice proceeded from between the two Cherubim, carved and gilded, affixed hovering over the cover of the Ark. This is an additional mystical meaning of the holy Cherubim, as they form a sacred channel of access to the deeper wisdom of God. A sound reason why they are called, "Streams of Wisdom."


### *Wisdom from the Holy Cherubim*

In April 2025 during contemplation after prayers, two angels appeared to me as I was meditating in the spiritual light. Each one of them grasped my arm and took me to a great cathedral-like hall, whose ceiling disappeared in the blur of its height. The walls towered until they were out of sight. There was an entrance door from which intense light issued forth. Through the doorway, we traveled down the tunnel of this light that emptied into a room like a smaller chapel. A brightly lit stained glass window was in the center of the wall, with a flaming diamond etched into it. The light shining through the glass was pure and clear. This stained glass symbolized the initiation of spiritual disciples on the path to God. The angels said, "You're in the Hall of Wisdom."

On a lectern there was a large holy book. I thought it was the Bible, but did not assume anything in these ventures with the holy angels. They said, "This is the highest book of holiness, higher than any book on Earth, because all wisdom in every culture precipitated from this book. It was written by the age-old Masters who passed it on to humanity out of their service to the Ancient of Days, from Whom the wisdom comes."

The angels added, "Also contained in this book are the sacred words for the rites of each sacred initiation a disciple (the Initiate) and the One Initiator (God) will speak."

I stumbled speaking to them but managed to ask if they were holy Seraphim. They said, "No, we are Cherubim. We hold the sacred wisdom, by the grace of God." I then asked about the holy Virtues, and they told me about them, which I include in that section of this book.

In parting, the Cherubim admonished and encouraged me to greater devotion to God, my holy family (Master Jesus and Mother Mary, et al), my brethren, and my religion. This intensity, they said, will bring about purification by design of my personal makeup. Devotion and wisdom are the keys to focus on this path.

# SONNET TO THE MOST HOLY CHERUBIM

Exalted fires, stellar winds gyrate

And blazing cities gild a cosmic lane

Where Cherubim hold close without a chain

Whose vibrant wings will lift and generate

The Wheel of Wisdom honed to navigate

That eons solve the destinies of pain

Salvation that was reckoned, evil slain

That all the holy angels consummate


We are Illumination from the Light

We drink the Streams of Wisdom from the Grail

We seek the imperfections blurring sight

We spark the fires when the winds exhale

In forges that create a heart contrite

From flaws that form the steppingstones and trail

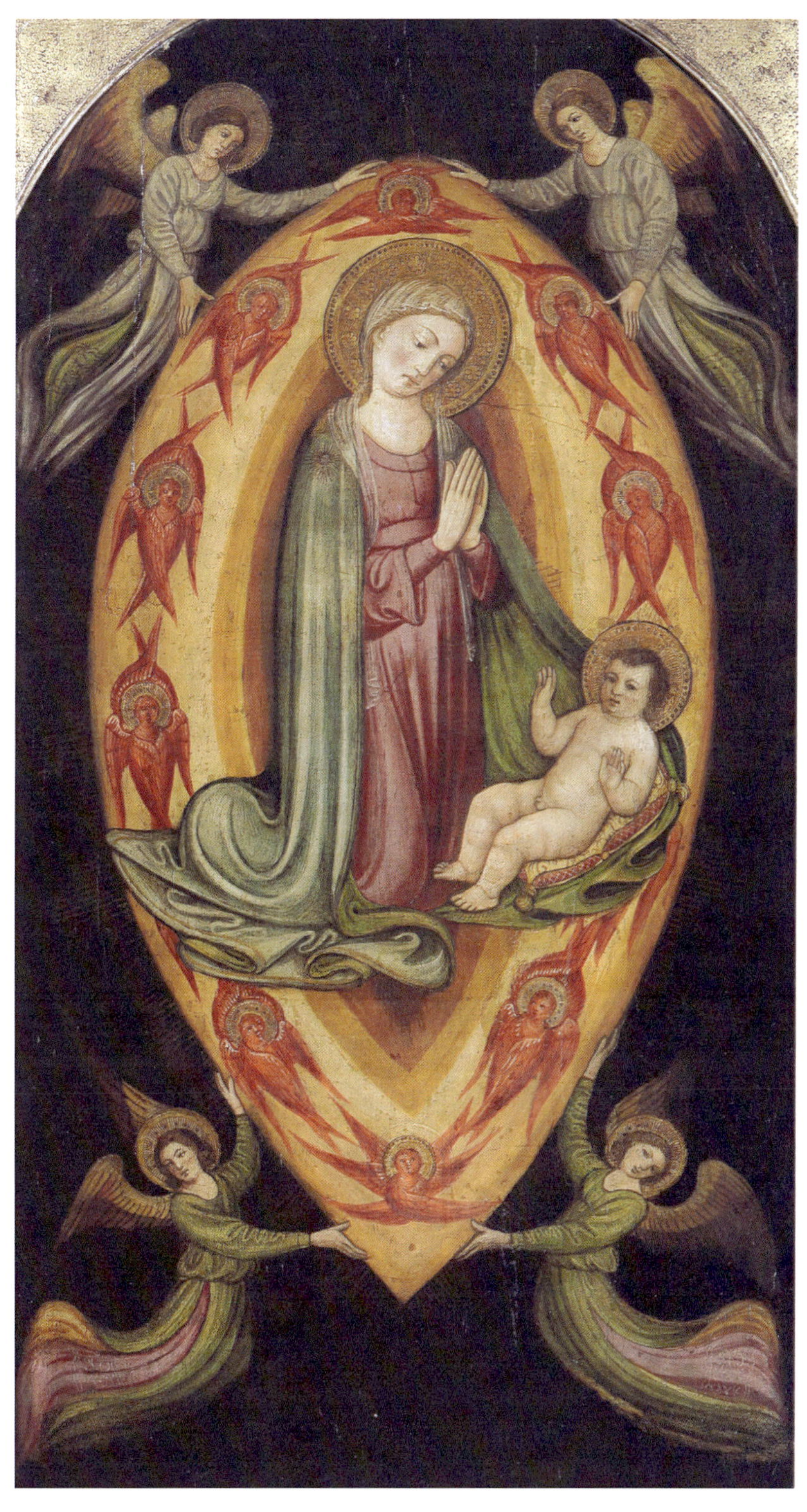

[10] Antonio di Maso, *The Madonna and Child*, c. 1450, London, Private Collection. *Courtesy of Artvee.com.*

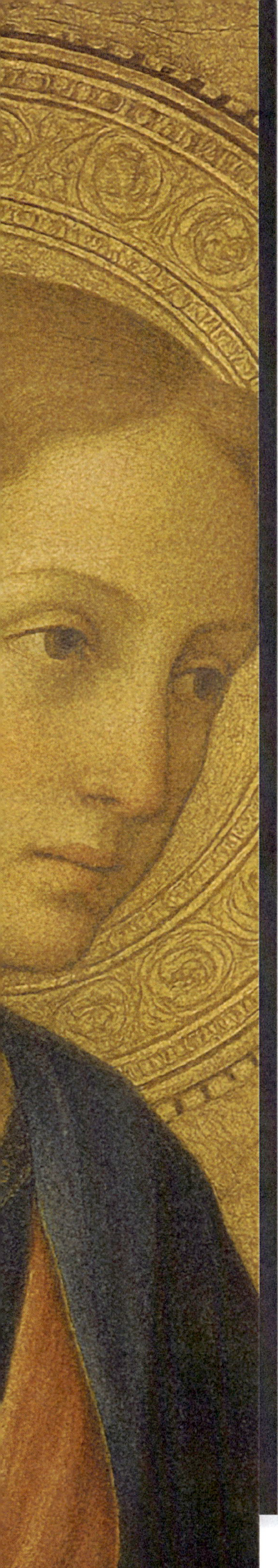



"The name of the most glorious and exalted Thrones denotes that which is exempt from and untainted by any base and earthly thing, and the supermundane ascent up the steep (way to God). For these have no part in that which is lowest, but dwell in fullest power, immovably and perfectly established in the Most High, and receive the Divine Immanence above all passion and matter, and manifest God, being attentively open to divine participations… Therefore the first Order of the holy Angels possesses above all others the characteristic of (spiritual)fire, and the abundant participation of Divine Wisdom, and the possession of the highest knowledge of the Divine Illuminations, and the characteristic of Thrones which symbolizes openness to the reception of God… For you will find that it (the symbol of fire) is used (in holy scriptures) not only under the figure of fiery wheels, but also of living creatures of fire, and of men flashing like lightning who heap live coals of fire about the Heavenly Beings, and of irresistibly rushing rivers of flame. Also it says that the Thrones are of fire… Whence it is clear that purification is assigned to the Thrones."[11]

"And roundabout were Seraphin, Cherubin, and Ophannin (Thrones): And these are they who sleep not and guard the throne of His glory."[12]

### *Wisdom from the Holy Throne*

During contemplation, I was shown an immense courtyard in a misty golden light. Classical buildings stood around it in a semicircle. Each building had Ionic columns, two on each side, upholding a simple pediment or gable roof. The area between the two sets of columns under the roof was shrouded in darkness, a

---

[11] Dionysius the Areopagite, *The Celestial Hierarchy.*
[12] *The Complete Book of Enoch.*

complete mystery. There was an angel with huge wings on the steps in front of one of these enormous buildings. I asked him his name.

He said, "Call me Throne."

He asked if I were ready, and I nodded affirmatively. He then took me away from there to another place with divine classical architecture. There was a beautiful white marble sepulcher with golden light shining from it. I asked him what it was.

The Throne said, "It is the sepulcher of your Beloved One."

Me: "Who is that?" (I was thinking, "Well, I love more than one.")

The Throne: "The one you know as Jesus. It is where He was temporarily laid. But because the Lord saw fit to bless it, it is now sacred. We Thrones hold sacred and protect all things touched by the Divine hand. Every major cathedral and temple on Earth the Divine God has consecrated, we watch over and bless with the divine fire.

Me: What about the smaller churches?

The Throne: They are assigned to the lesser angels to take care of…We are finished for today.

THE MOST HOLY THRONE

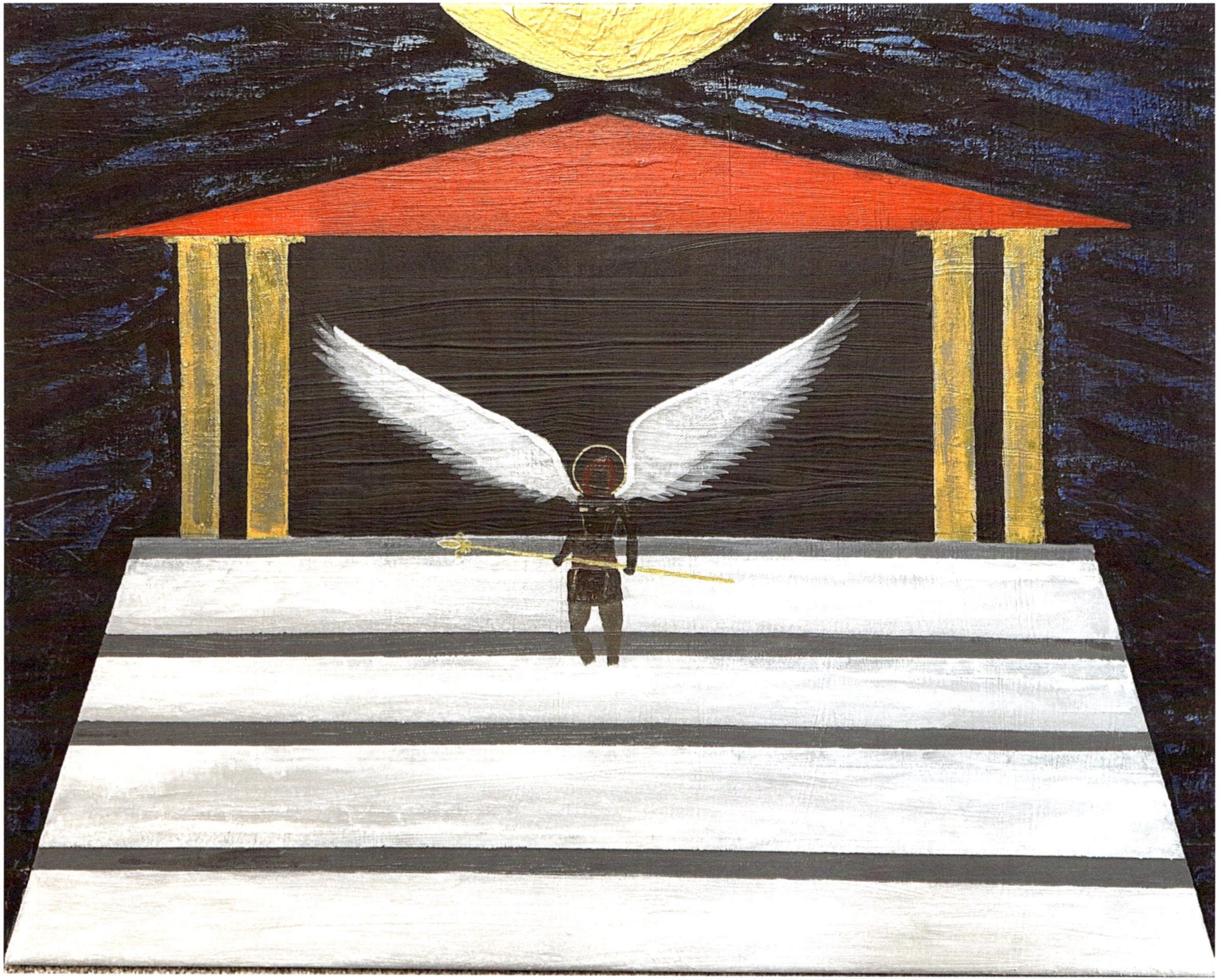

# SONNET TO THE MOST HOLY THRONES

When I beheld the grandeur of the Thrones
I'd known the whir of bees who guard the hive
And crosshairs used by golden hawks that dive
And Light that dashes inner temple stones
In place of olden sacrificial bones
My altars are of incense burning live
And pluming to the sky with prayers that I've
Laid down in clouds the highest priest atones

Elysian Thrones are pure and fear no thing
Divine cathedrals stream their holy fire
Their wings, the breadth of oaks, are for the King
And lesser duties call upon a squire
The Thrones have sworn to bear a noble ring
As Sentries of the Flame who never tire

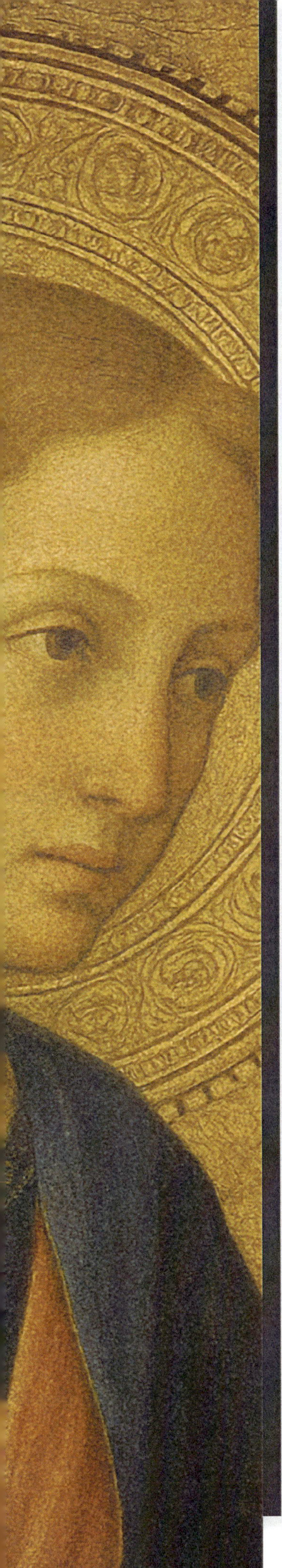



"As Dionysius says (Div. Nom. xii): 'Dominion is attributed to God in a special manner, by way of excess: but the Divine word gives the more illustrious heavenly princes the name of Lord by participation, through whom the inferior angels receive the Divine gifts.' Hence Dionysius also states (Coel. Hier. viii) that the name 'Domination' means first 'a certain liberty, free from servile condition and common subjection, such as that of plebeians, and from tyrannical oppression,' endured sometimes even by the great. Secondly, it signifies 'a certain rigid and inflexible supremacy which does not bend to any servile act, or to the act, of those who are subject to or oppressed by tyrants.' Thirdly, it signifies 'the desire and participation of the true dominion which belongs to God.' Likewise the name of each order signifies the participation of what belongs to God; for example, as the name 'Virtues' signifies the participation of the Divine virtue; and the same principle applies to the rest. The names 'Domination,' 'Power,' and 'Principality' belong to government in different ways. The place of a lord is only to prescribe what is to be done, so Gregory says (Hom. xxiv in Evang.), that 'some companies of the angels, because others are subject to obedience to them, are called dominations."[13]

"The name given to the holy Dominions signifies, I think, a certain unbounded elevation to that which is above, freedom from all that is of the earth, and from all inward inclination to the bondage of discord, a liberal superiority to harsh tyranny, an exemptness from degrading servility and from all that is low: for they are untouched by any inconsistency. They are true Lords, perpetually aspiring to true lordship, and to the Source of lordship, and they providentially fashion themselves and those below them, as far as possible, into the likeness

[13] Aquinas, *Summa Theologica, Article 108.*

of true lordship. They do not turn towards vain shadows, but wholly give themselves to that true Authority, forever one with the Godlike Source of lordship."[14]

Dominations or Dominions are responsible for leading the lower angelic orders as well. They enforce the law of God on Earth. Dominions, in terms of limits, ensure none below them overstep their area of responsibility, either energetically or personally. Every angelic order and sub-order has an area of responsibility and the dominions ensure that the domains are kept intact and forbids any trespassing or "overflow" from others.

---

[14] Dionysius the Areopagite, *The Celestial Hierarchy.*

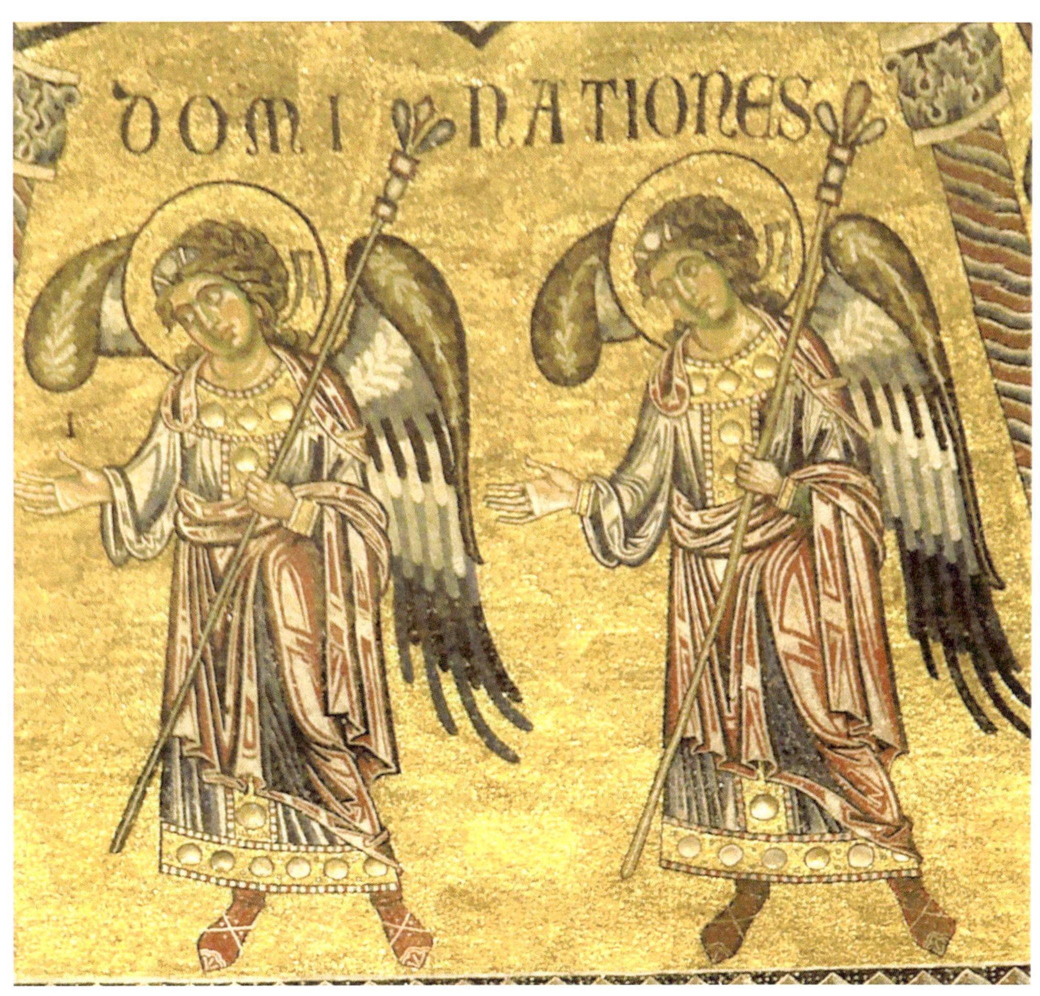



[15] Meliore di Jacopo and Coppo di Marcovaldo, *Angelic Hierarchy, Dominions*, mosaic, c. 1260, Baptistery San Giovanni, Florence, *Courtesy Wikimedia Commons,* Photo by Matthias Kabel, Cropped by Sailko, Licensed under GFDL, https://commons.wikimedia.org/wiki/File:Mosaici_del_battistero,_angeli,_dominazioni.jpg#Licensing. Accessed 6 March 2025.

# SONNET TO THE MOST HOLY DOMINIONS

A boundless reach of Light is bent by you

Beyond our ken, our earthly lives ignored

For you but wield the right of any lord

To govern many skies, should God accrue

Your sole dominion is a lordship's due

That I shall know by destiny's award

Whose holy river leads me to a fjord

Where eagles reap a wind I never knew


You bind apocalypse in silent ways

For yours is not a yoke that bondage buys

But effort is the muscle that will raise

A soul to life above the fruitless cries

And there the vision of your lavish haze

Of humble deeds that shine before our eyes

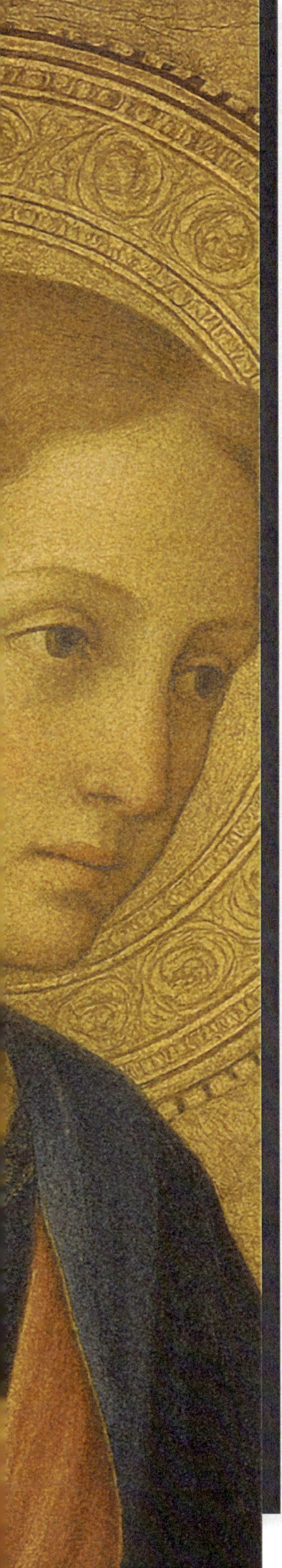



"The name of the holy Powers, co-equal with the divine Dominions and Virtues, signifies an orderly and unconfined order in the divine receptions, and the regulation of intellectual and supermundane power which never debases its authority by tyrannical force, but is irresistibly urged onward in due order to the Divine. It beneficently leads those below it, as far as possible, to the Supreme Power, which is the Source of Power, which it manifests after the manner of Angels in the well-ordered ranks of its own authoritative power. This middle rank of the Celestial Intelligences, having these Godlike characteristics, is purified, illuminated and perfected in the manner already described, by the divine Illuminations bestowed upon it in a secondary manner through the first hierarchical Order, and shown forth in a secondary manifestation by the middle choir."[16]

"The name 'Power' points out a kind of order, according to what the Apostle says, 'He that resisteth the power, resisteth the ordination of God' (Romans 13:2). And so Dionysius says (Coel. Hier. viii) that the name 'Power' signifies a kind of ordination both as regards the reception of Divine things, and as regards the Divine actions performed by superiors towards inferiors by leading them to things above. Therefore, to the order of 'Powers' it belongs to regulate what is to be done by those who are subject to them."[17]

The holy Powers are "a wheelhouse" responsible for distributing and stepping down the higher frequency fires of energy to the Virtues, Principalities, Archangels, and Angels. The transferring of divine energies is a science unto itself. The Powers hold the unique rank of the middle position of the middle triad, thus occupying the central location of the entire advanced hierarchy.

[16] Dionysius the Areopagite, *The Celestial Hierarchy.*
[17] Aquinas, *Summa Theologica, Article 108.*

Additionally they are the liaison betwixt the Dominions and Virtues in their own triad. This gives them the unique position to fully contain their activities (i.e., no human contact) within the hierarchy. They occupy a pivotal fulcrum, as such, within the angelic ranks.

# SONNET TO THE MOST HOLY POWERS

Celestial Powers yield to power's grace
And those illumined ones, the guides of men
Have purified my angel's heart again
For I must reach perfection for my race
But no intelligence can measure space
Nor fences mark the limits of my pen
Thus union with Enlightenment is when
The universe compresses in my place

No borders and no locks to your domain
The scions of the Powers shall be heir
The royalty of power rules the plane
As sons of God whom Spirit-Matter bear
The Limitless the Logos will explain
Expressing through the Powers everywhere

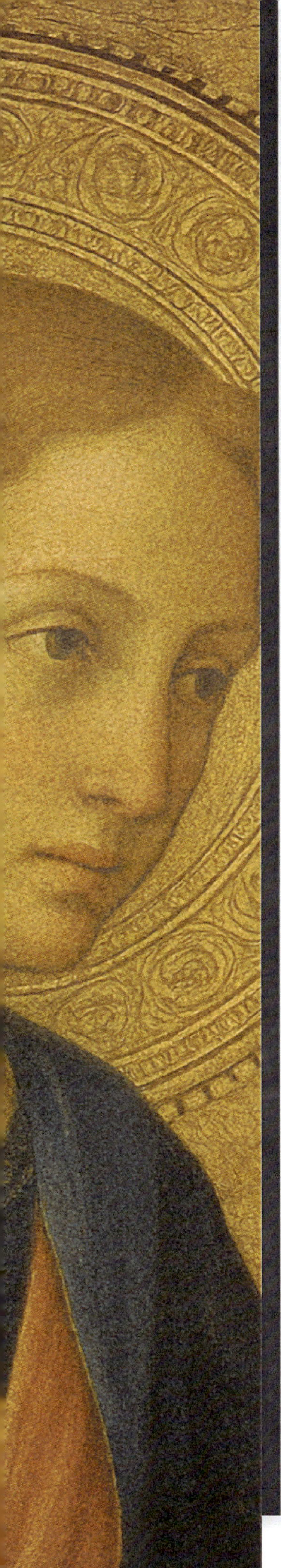

"*V*irtue can be taken in two ways. First, commonly, considered as the medium between the essence and the operation, and in that sense all the heavenly spirits are called heavenly virtues, as also 'heavenly essences.' Secondly, as meaning a certain excellence of strength; and thus it is the proper name of an angelic order. Hence Dionysius says (Coel. Hier. viii) that the name 'virtues' signifies a certain virile and immovable strength; first, in regard of those Divine operations which befit them; secondly, in regard to receiving Divine gifts. Thus it signifies that they undertake fearlessly the Divine behests appointed to them; and this seems to imply strength of mind."[18]

"The name of the holy Virtues signifies a certain powerful and unshakable virility welling forth into all their Godlike energies; not being weak and feeble for any reception of the divine Illuminations granted to it, mounting upwards in fullness of power to an assimilation with God; never falling away from the Divine Life through its own weakness, but ascending unwaveringly to the superessential Virtue which is the Source of virtue: fashioning itself, as far as it may, in virtue; perfectly turned towards the Source of virtue, and flowing forth providentially to those below it, abundantly filling them with virtue."[19]

The holy Virtues carry out the directions of the Dominions. Virtues are responsible for maintaining the equilibrium which is usually peace and harmony between and within communities and between nations. And outside humanity, the same balance applies to the lower animal and plant kingdoms.

The holy Virtues distribute the intelligence and knowledge to the orders below them, and ensure the highest sanctity and holiness maintained in the

---

[18] Aquinas, *Summa Theologica, Article 108*.
[19] Dionysius the Areopagite, *The Celestial Hierarchy*.

reception and obeisance of that knowledge, so that no distortion enters into its purposes for and in use by the lower orders.

# SONNET TO THE MOST HOLY VIRTUES

The Logos opens worlds by Trinity

And outer space, the changing room of fire

Across the sky the Solar Ones conspire

The vast of whirls to lord reality

Unspeakable, they gild eternity

Pure lives display the cosmic life by pyre

Whose holy will the Word shall speak and sire

That Virtues brace untold divinity


The slingshot of a virtue powers flight

A soaring that is not so haven-bound

The Order of the Virtues is my plight

A destination Spirit spirals round

For God creates their essence from the Light

Immovable and virile to be crowned

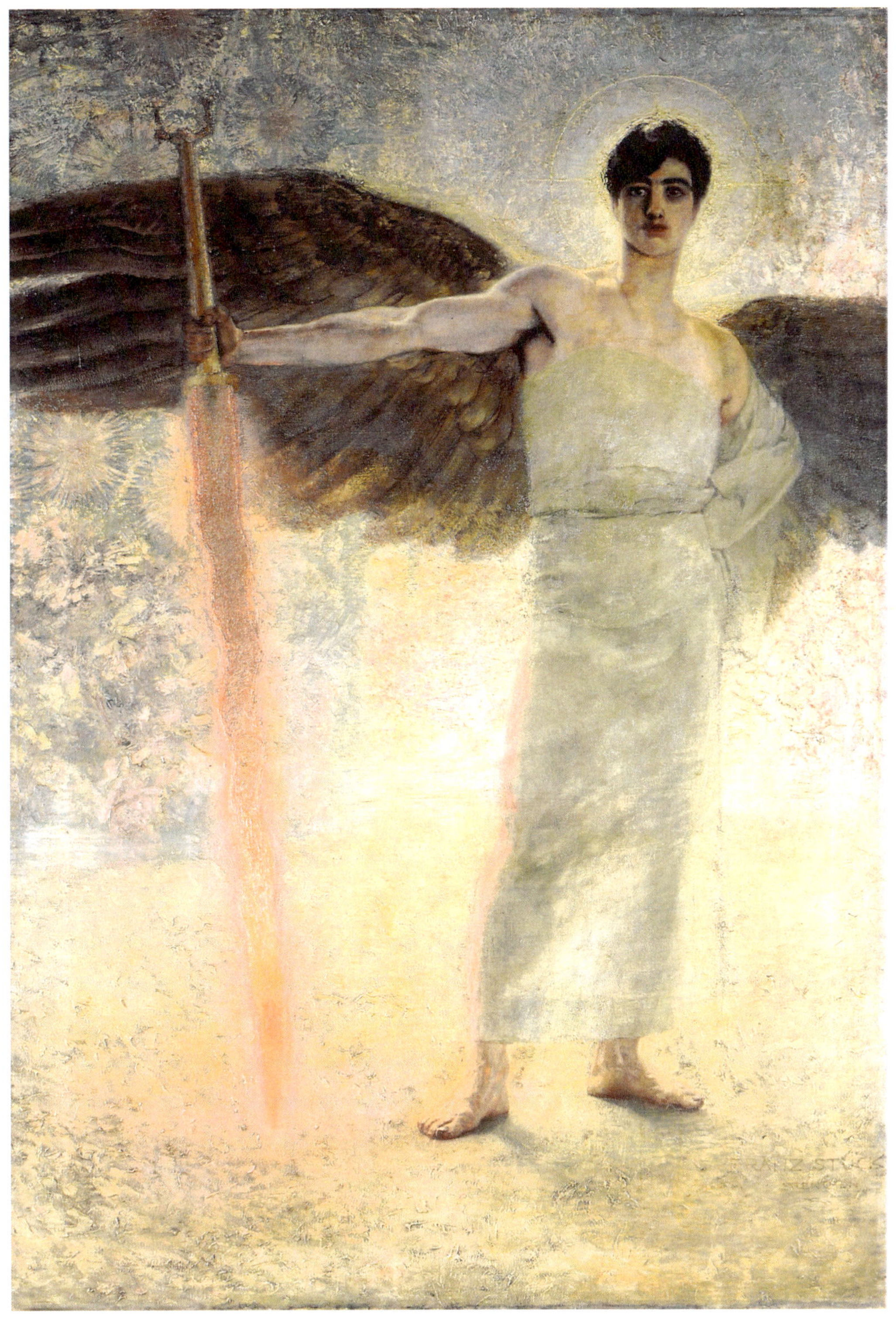

[20] Franz von Stuck, *The Guardian of Paradise*, 1889, Museum Villa Stuck, Munich. *Courtesy of Artvee.com.*

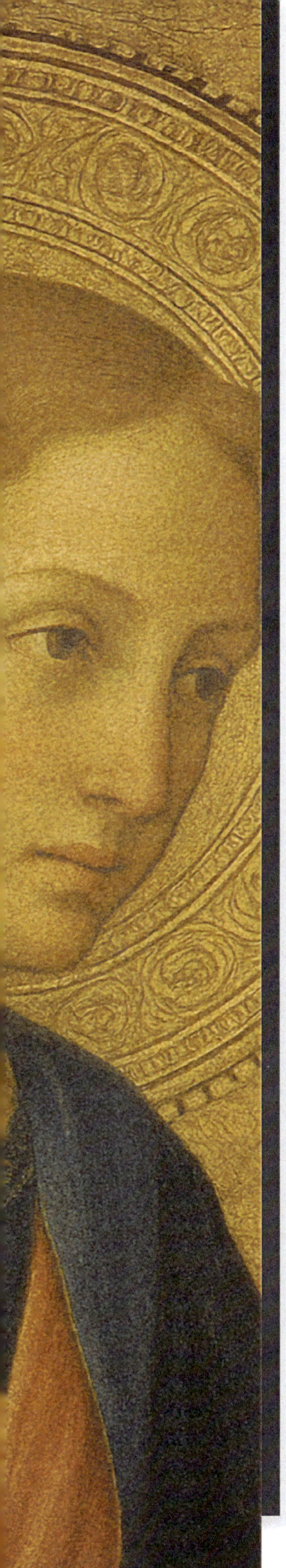



"The name of the Celestial Principalities signifies their Godlike princeliness and authoritativeness in an Order which is holy and most fitting to the princely Powers, and that they are wholly turned towards the Prince of Princes, and lead others in princely fashion, and that they are formed, as far as possible, in the likeness of the Source of Principality, and reveal

Its superessential order by the good Order of the princely Powers."[21]

"To preside [principari] as Gregory says (Hom. xxiv in Ev.) is 'to be first among others,' as being first in carrying out what is ordered to be done. And so Dionysius says (Coel. Hier. ix) that the name of 'Principalities' signifies 'one who leads in a sacred order.' For those who lead others, being first among them, are properly called 'princes,' according to the words, 'The princes went before, the singers followed after' (Psalm 68:25)."[22]

The holy Principalities or Princedoms minister to cities and towns, states and provinces.

---

[21] Dionysius the Areopagite, *The Celestial Hierarchy.*

[22] Aquinas, *Summa Theologica, Article 108.*

# SONNET TO THE MOST HOLY PRINCEDOMS

Shall I traverse your princedom on my way?

I'm searching for a treasure of much worth

By lone crusade, as knight of modest birth

Yet under desert sun's unholy ray

I need a Prince whom I'll not have to pay

Who walks as high as eagles wheel from earth

Where hapless denizens mine gold in dearth

And so I plead, O Prince of grand array

This sacred order for the Prince of Peace

Should not forget how low is my estate

The road is long and thirst is my caprice

The wine of wisdom filled my cup so late

I do not wish to spill a drop nor cease

To bear my gift of love from God innate

SAINT BRIGID AND THE MYSTICAL FIRE

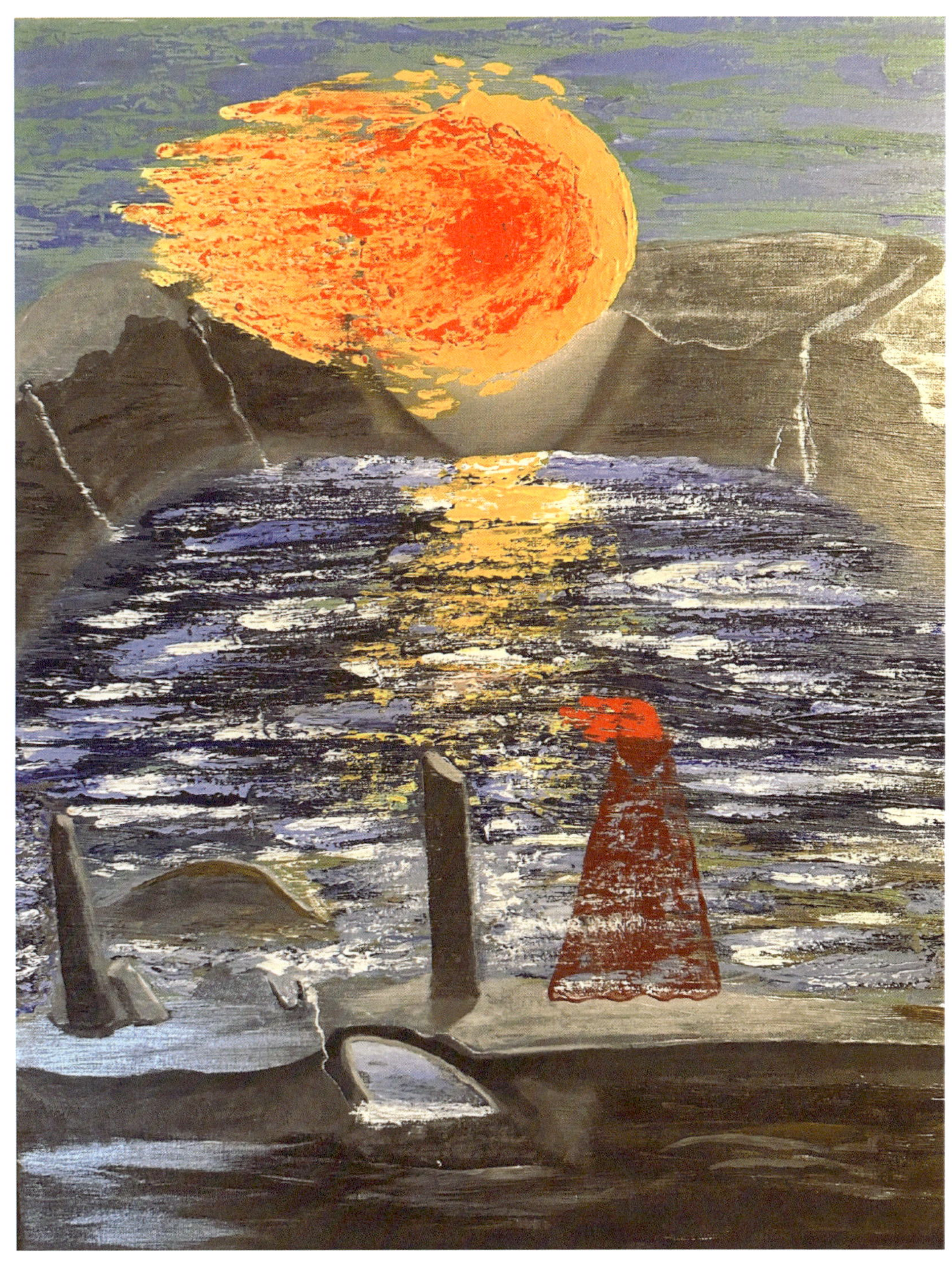

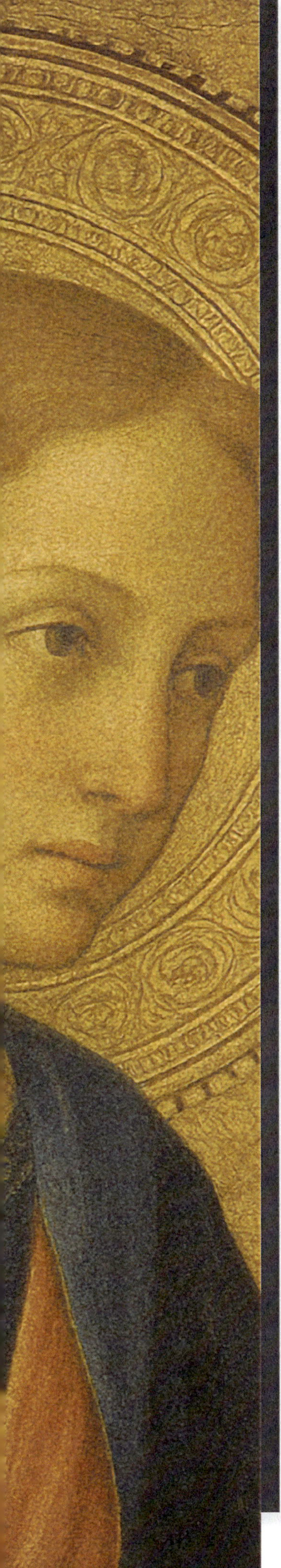



"The choir of the holy Archangels is placed in the same threefold Order as the Celestial Principalities: for, as has been said, there is one Hierarchy and Order which includes these and the Angels. But since each Hierarchy has first, middle and last ranks, the holy Order of Archangels, through its middle position, participates in the two extremes, being joined with the most holy Principalities and with the holy Angels."

"It is joined with the Princedoms because it is turned in a princely way to the superessential Principality and, as far as it can attain, molds itself in His likeness, and it is seen to be the cause of the union of the Angels with its own orderly and invisible leadership. It is joined with the Angels because it belongs to the interpreting Order, receiving in its turn the illuminations from the First Powers, and beneficently announcing these revelations to the Angels: and by means of the Angels, it shows them forth to us in the measure of the mystical receptivity of each one who is inspired by the divine Illumination. For the Angels, as we have said, fill up and complete the lowest choir of all the Hierarchies of the Celestial Intelligences since they are the last of the Celestial Beings possessing the angelic nature. And they, indeed, are more properly named Angels by us than are those of a higher rank because their choir is more directly in contact with manifested and mundane things."[23]

The Eastern Catholic/Orthodox and Roman Catholic churches combine up to seven names of archangels in scriptural canon. The Roman Church discourages naming any angels except the three mentioned in Roman canonical scripture: Saints Michael, Gabriel, and Raphael. Other Christian denominations have variations of these names, some extending to eight in number, as in the Coptic Christian Church. In the Eastern Orthodox and Byzantine Catholic traditions,

[23] Dionysius the Areopagite, *The Celestial Hierarchy.*

Archangel Uriel is commemorated on a feast day called the "Synaxis of the Archangel Michael and Other Bodiless Powers" on November 8. The Orthodox churches of Egypt and Ethiopia, Christians celebrate July 28 in honor of the Archangel Uriel.[24] Because the Archangel Uriel is venerated by so many denominations, he is included in this book. Those traditions include:

- St. Uriel's Episcopal Church, Sea Girt, New Jersey
- Eastern Orthodoxy
- Eastern (Byzantine) Catholicism
- Anglicanism
- Rabbinic Judaism
- Oriental Orthodoxy
- Lutheranism
- Esoteric Christianity[25]

"And these are the names of the holy angels who watch mankind.
Uriel, one of the holy angels, who is over the world and over Tartarus."[26]

On a grand scale, nations are assigned guiding angels.

When the Most High allotted each nation its heritage,
when he separated out human beings,
He set up the boundaries of the peoples
after the number of the divine beings (angels).
(Deuteronomy 32:8-9)

According to the *Book of Daniel* 10:13 and 12:1, Archangel Michael the Prince is the guardian/guide for the Hebrews for that time period in the Old Testament. They administer divine energies to small or large groups of humans as one of their duties. The Celtic nations are a salient example of a culture which claims guardianship on land and sea from the great Archangel Michael. In the Revelation 1:11, the Apostle John is directed to write to the angels of the seven churches of that time, which were in seven cities of the Roman Empire in present

[24] Matthew Bunson, *Angels A to Z: A Who's Who of the Heavenly Host* (New York: Potter/Ten Speed/Harmony/Rodale, 2010), p. 103.
[25] Wikipedia Contributors, *Uriel*, Wikipedia, The Free Encyclopedia, Accessed 2 February 2025. https://en.wikipedia.org/wiki/Uriel.
[26] *The Complete Book of Enoch.*

day Turkey. The Hierarchs (religious leaders) of these cities were guided by the angels. Those letters start with *Revelation Chapter 2.*

"Pharaoh was shown through visions by the Angel who presided over the Egyptians, and the Prince of Babylon was shown by his own Angel, the watchful and overruling Power of Providence. And for those nations the servants of the true God were appointed as leaders, the interpretations of angelic visions having been revealed from God through angels to holy men near to the angels, like Daniel and Joseph."[27]

This method of choosing a nation's leader from the most virtuous, spiritually advanced is the true divine royal lineage and comprised the original Law of Divine Right, later distorted to human bloodline and abased through time.

---

[27] Dionysius the Areopagite, *The Celestial Hierarchy.*

"And then Michael, Uriel, Raphael, and Gabriel looked down from
heaven and saw much blood being shed upon the earth, and
all lawlessness being wrought upon the earth."[29]

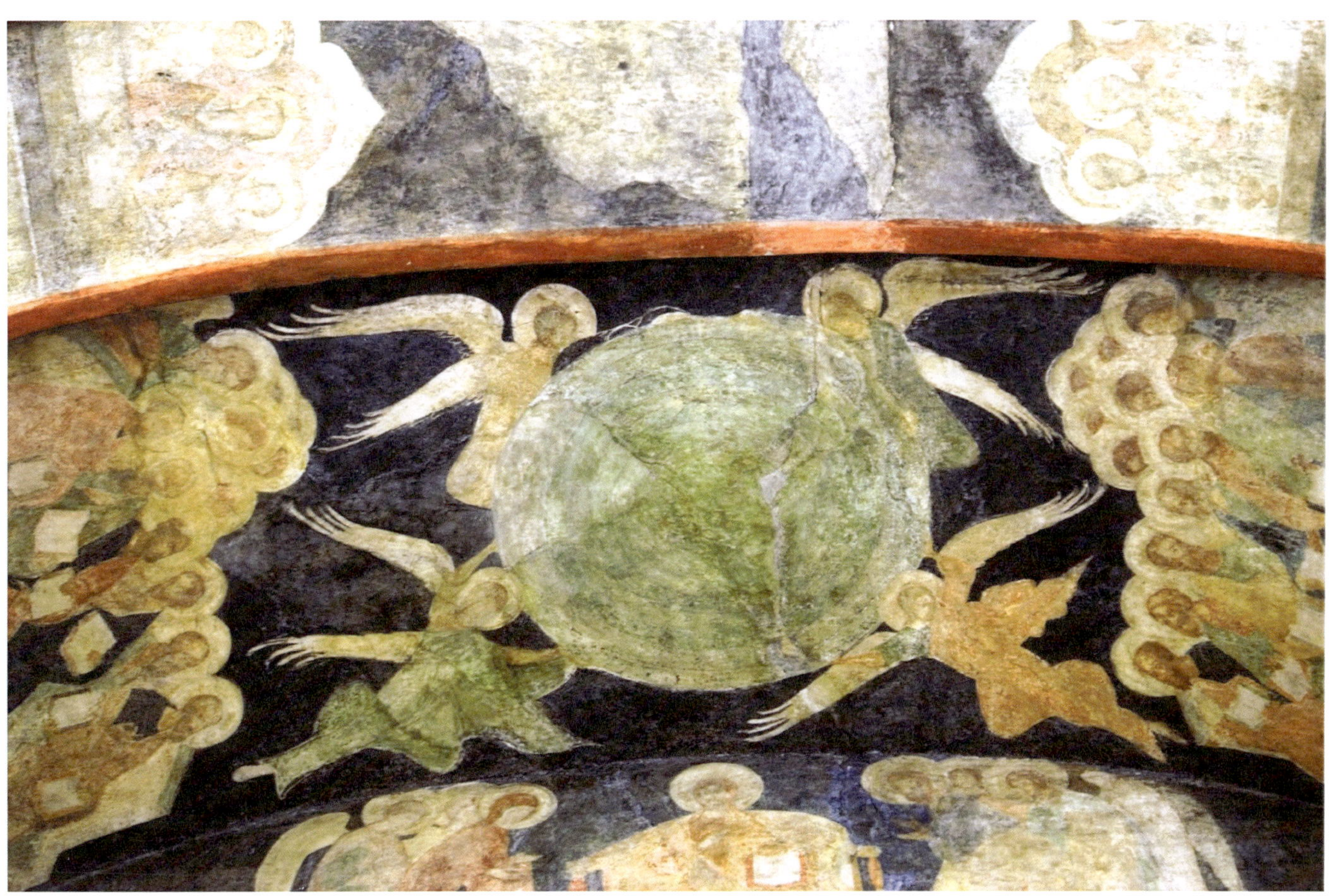

[28] Contributing Artists, *Archangels on Saint Basil's Cathedral Façade*, Kremlin, Moscow,
Courtesy *ID90873357© Ekaterina Bykova, Dreamstime.com.*
[29] *The Complete Book of Enoch.*

The captains of the holy army swore

To flank in valor *He Who Ever Was*

They stand the gates of heaven under laws

Divinity had forged from molten core

From oracle of God They will restore

The boundary where evil has to pause

Enforcing all decrees from that First Cause

From throne to footstool Who obey and war


And when the royal fiefdom they must rule

Through cycles that outlast a nation's trace

Shall graduate from Wisdom's ancient school

The dawn will gloss humanity's old face

Who started up this mount as loaded mule

But then a steed of splendor glowing grace

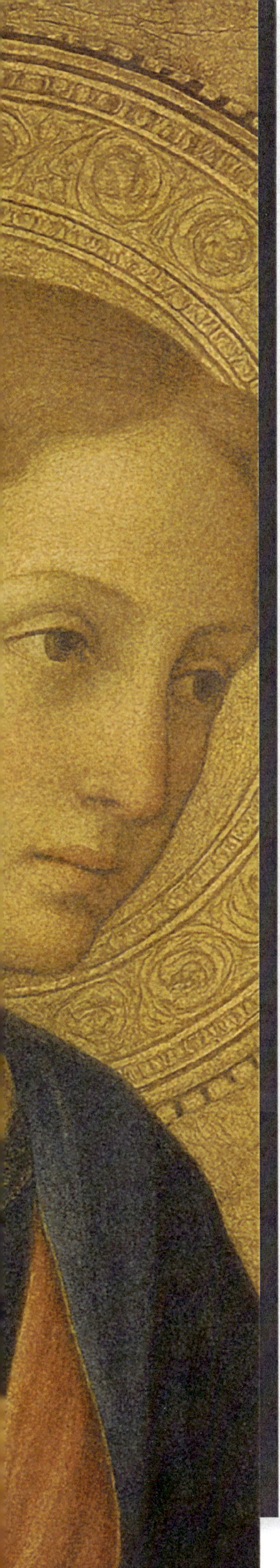



Michael: "Who is like unto God?"

"Yet the Archangel Michael, when he argued with the devil in a dispute over the body of Moses, did not venture to pronounce a reviling judgment upon him but said, 'May the Lord rebuke you!'"
(Jude 1:9)

"At that time there shall arise Michael, the great prince, guardian of your people; It shall be a time unsurpassed in distress since the nation began until that time. At that time your people shall escape, everyone who is found written in the book."                     (Daniel 12:1)

"And the angel Michael seized me by my right hand and lifted me up and led me forth into all the secrets, and he showed me all the secrets of righteousness. And he showed me all the secrets of the ends of the heaven, and all the chambers of all the stars, and all the luminaries, whence they proceed before the face of the holy ones. And he translated my spirit into the heaven of heavens, and I saw there as it were a structure built of crystals and between those crystals tongues of living fire."[30]

The evolutionary line of Archangel Michael and his fellow archangels is connected in power and evolution to the Seven Spirits Who Stand before the Throne. It takes eons and great sacrifice over time to attain that level, the next major level for them.

Interestingly, Skellig Michael, an island of sky-piercing rock off the southwest coast of Ireland, Saint Michael's Mount in Cornwall, and Mont-Saint-Michel in Brittany form a ley line of monasteries dedicated to Archangel Michael. These three sanctuaries are a clear expression of the faith of the Celtic Christians who garnered, through devotion, the protection of Saint Michael on land and sea.

[30] *The Complete Book of Enoch.*

Amazingly, this line of sanctuaries, which varies an average of 27 km between sites, flows all the way to Stella Maris Monastery on Mount Carmel, Israel, as it crosses two more sacred sites in Italy and one in Greece, each dedicated in some way to Saint Michael, to form the line or "Sword of Saint Michael."

# MAP OF THE SWORD OF SAINT MICHAEL[31]

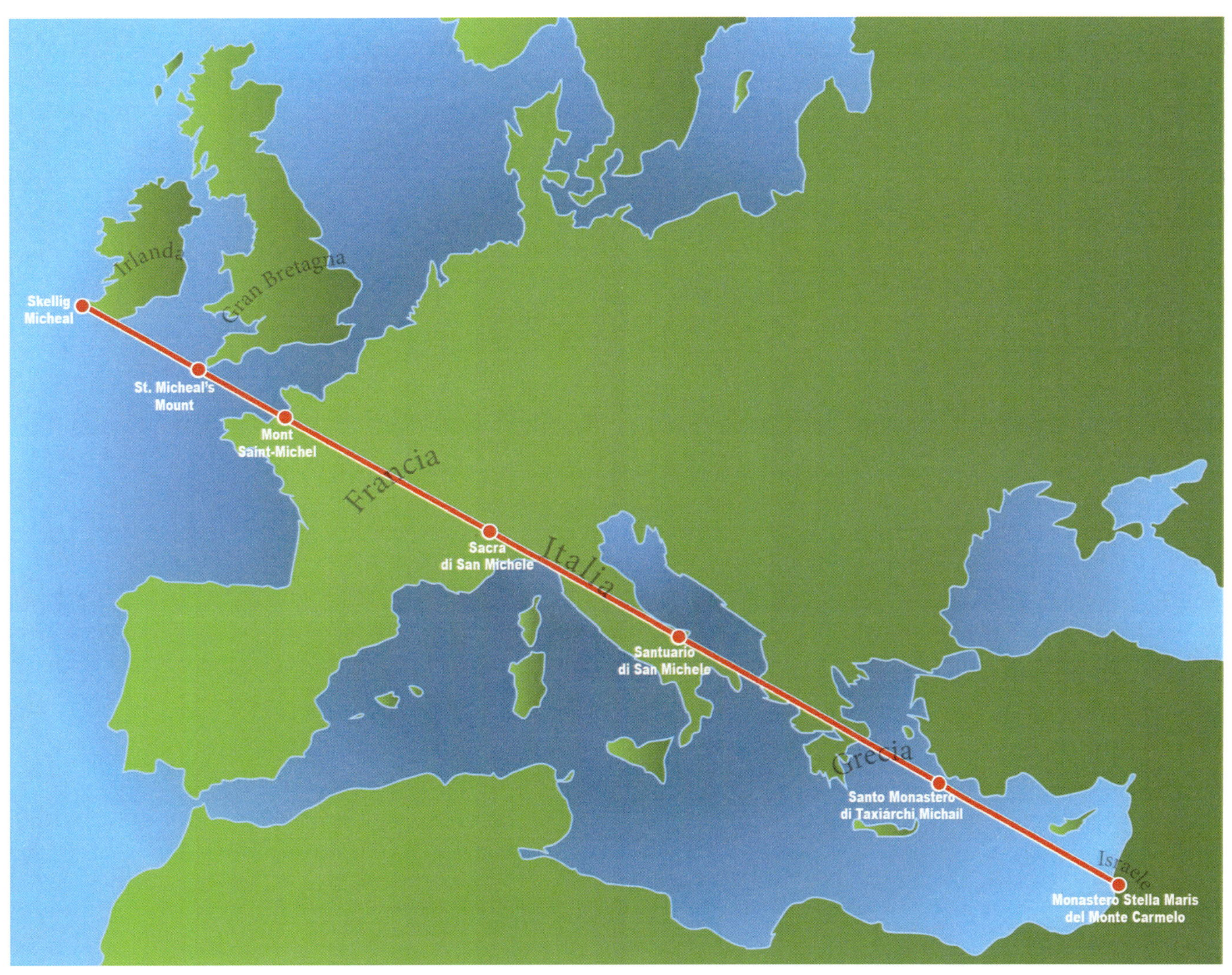




[31] Enryonthecloud, *The Sword of Saint Michael*, own work (based on Google Map), Public Domain, Wikimedia Commons, https://commons.wikimedia.org/w/index.php?curid=62372148, Accessed 01/12/25.

SONNET FOR SAINT MICHAEL THE ARCHANGEL

My brother Michael captains winged gendarmes

With rapid power crushes he the blight

Fidelity in righteousness brings might

Saint Michael shields the weak from one who harms

Amidst the human clamor that alarms

The guideposts of a nation he will right

And press the steady course with line of sight

To lead the legions of the souls-in-arms


He is a son, yet he's no son alone

The heaven-bound recite his holy cry

Humility is strength he'll ever own

Devotion pure and holy never die

El Shaddai dwells where winds have never blown

His lightning-sword through Michael none defy

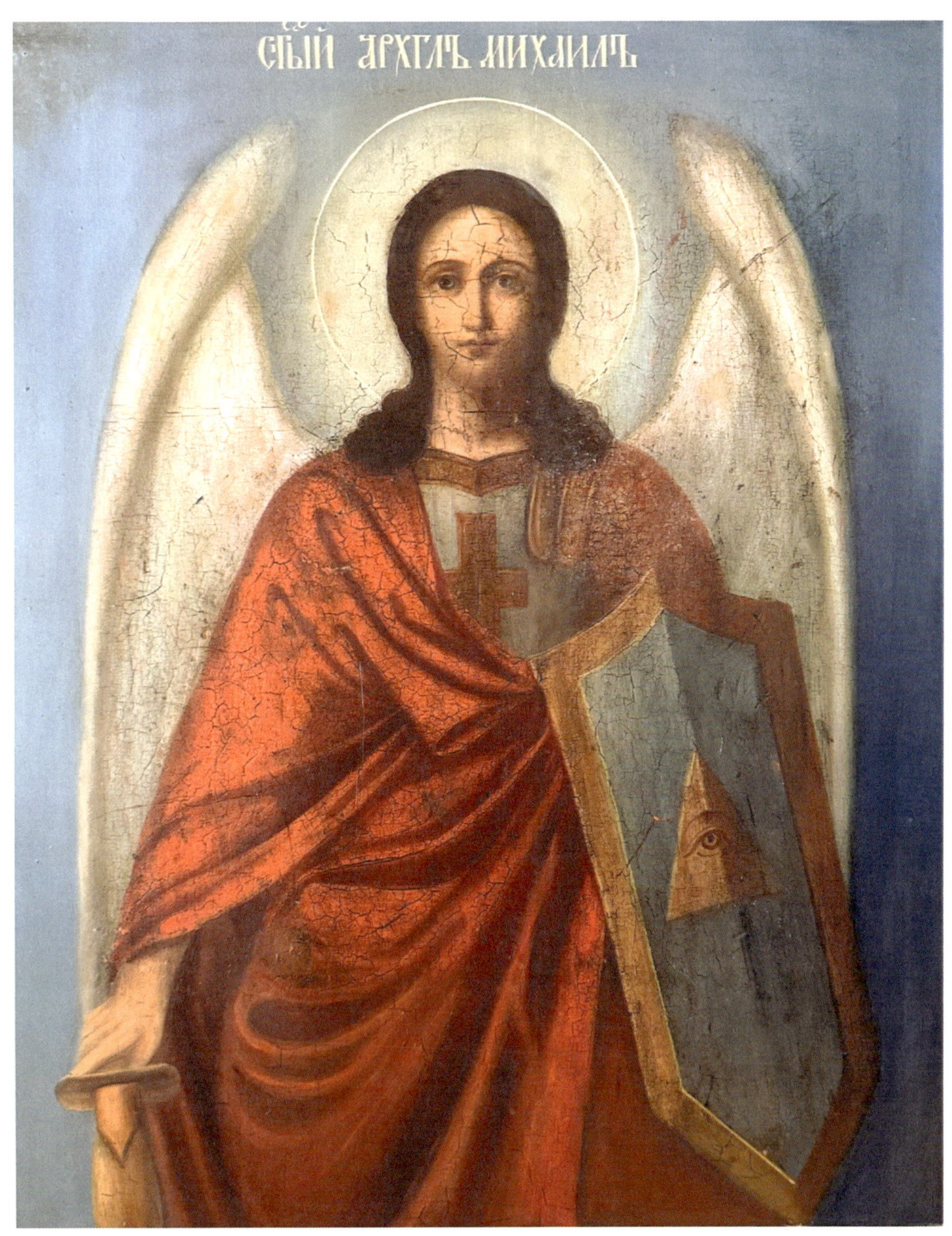



[32] Artist unknown, *Archangel Michael, (oil on wood)*, c.1860, Private collection, salvaged from an Orthodox church in the Holy Land, Israel.

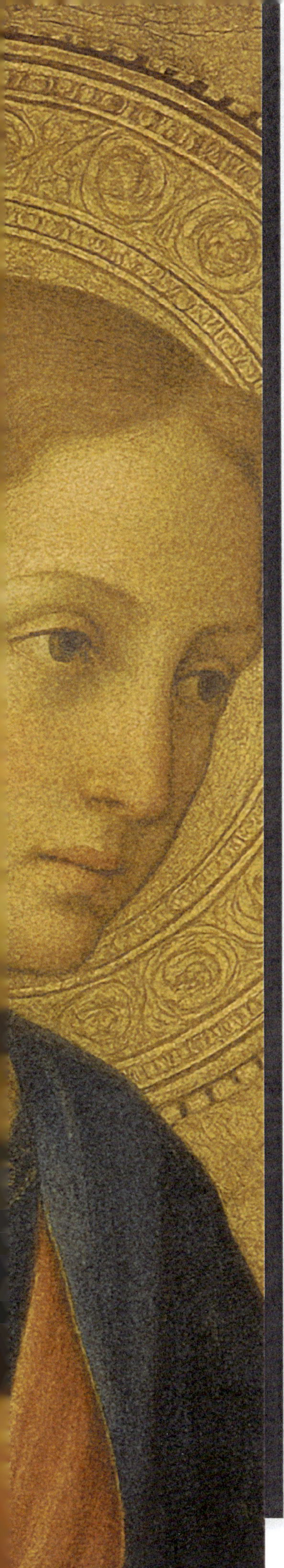



*I*n August of 2020, during deep contemplation I saw a spirit who was dressed like a man in a long white shirt waving to me to come to him. He was insistent! So I followed him across an ethereal field and over a knoll where appeared a small white house. He pointed to it, as the inner sun shone brightly upon it. He said, "Go there."

I arrived at the porch and sat on a chair facing the sun. I asked, "What am I supposed to do here?"

I was told by a holy saint who was nearby to wait. I was actually wanting to go to sleep in my physical-plane room in my house. It was late. But I was encouraged by this saint to persevere, remain alert, and "standby." Then the man who'd waved to me reappeared to alert me that someone was coming. Soon, a man with a red fleur-de-lis on the front of his medieval outfit approached me on the porch. He asked if he could have a seat. I said, "Yes" and waved my hand toward a chair. I asked him who he was.

He said, "I am Saint Michael. Do you know why I have come?" He didn't give me any time to adjust and acknowledge his divine personage.

I said, "No."

He continued, "I have come to give you My blessing. Stand up." I did.

"You, I, and Saint Illtyd are warriors. And from the Blessed Light comes the Army of God. You are now a soldier in that army of the Most High. He then pulled out this huge, marvelous sword and tapped me on my two shoulders and forehead, saying, "In the name of the Father, and the Son, and the Holy Spirit."

I dropped to my knees out of deep respect and spiritual humility to this great spiritual Being.

Saint Michael then spoke, "We are now close brothers. Whenever you need my help, you only need to call my name, and/or think of me, and I will be there to protect you."

I thanked him for this astonishing gift of friendship, still confounded as to how I could warrant such a gift. I recalled just that day having inserted the image of my painting of Saint Michael into the Celtic Mystics manuscript I was working on.

Then he said, "Do you have any questions for me before I go?"

I asked him for a favor which had to do with an icon that I had of him. (The icon's image adjoins this article). He said he would grant me the favor, and it came to pass some weeks later. As he said goodbye, I thanked him, and he waved his hand out toward the Light, and his winged white horse, Brian, appeared out of the bright glow. He hopped on Brian and rode away in a flash of light! Brian the holy steed is an angelic projection of Saint Michael, well-known in Celtic lore. And beloved Saint Michael as a divine archangel has this knowledge and power.

After this meeting, life continued to take on a completely different reality, as did my perception of the spiritual reality of this world, and my life within it. I found the spiritual reality more reliable, though I did not beckon Saint Michael needlessly. Indeed, I was reeling in the wonders of God's providence, Whose mercy endures forever.

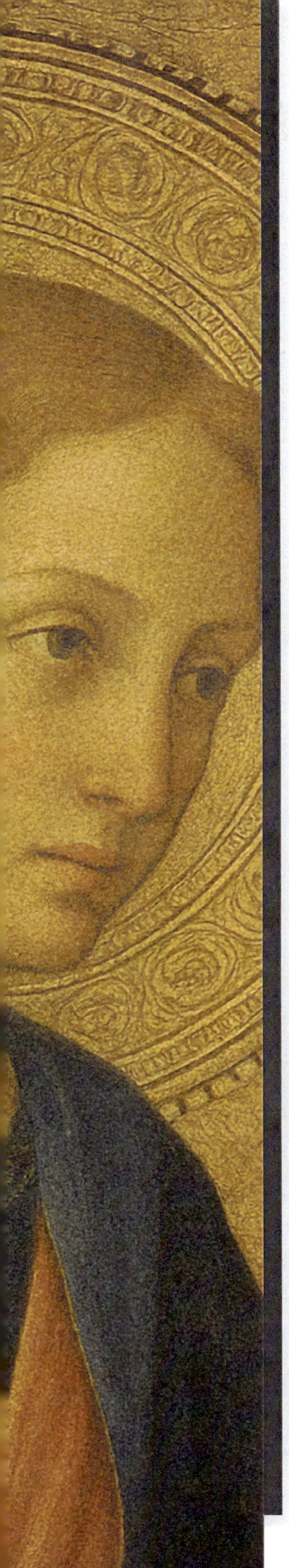



*G*abriel: "God is my strength" or "Hero of God"

"In the sixth month, the angel Gabriel was sent from God to a town of Galilee called Nazareth, to a virgin betrothed to a man named Joseph, of the house of David, and the virgin's name was Mary. And coming to her, he said, 'Hail, favored one! The Lord is with you.'" (Luke 1:26-28)

"And these are the names of the holy angels who watch mankind… Gabriel, one of the holy angels, who is over Paradise and the serpents and the Cherubim…And the third voice I heard pray and intercede for those who dwell on the earth and supplicate in the name of the Lord of Spirits…and who is set over all the powers, is Gabriel."[33]

Saint Gabriel the Archangel is further written about in sacred Jewish literature, Rabbinic Judaism, the Kabbalah and the Jewish Bible of the Old Testament.

Archangel Gabriel appears to Zechariah, the father-to-be of John the Baptist, and brings him a message of good news about the conceiving of his elderly wife Elizabeth. But Zechariah's disbelief brings this response from Saint Gabriel:

"Then Zechariah said to the angel, "How shall I know this? For I am an old man, and my wife is advanced in years." And the angel said to him in reply, "I am Gabriel, who stand before God. I was sent to speak to you and to announce to you this good news.  But now you will be speechless and unable to talk until the day these things take place, because you did not believe my words, which will be fulfilled at their proper time." (Luke 1:18-20)

In the 10th Century, Archangel Gabriel also appeared in the guise of a monk to a disciple in a hermitage on Mount Athos, Greece and miraculously inscribed the words of a hymn to Mother Mary, the Theotokos, on a piece of slate with

---

[33] *The Complete Book of Enoch.*

His finger. He then vanished. The hymn soon began to be chanted in all the churches in the Divine Liturgy. That sacred place is now called Adein.

In the Hebrew Bible's *Book of Daniel*, Saint Gabriel appears to the prophet Daniel to explain his visions.

The Islamic Koran conveys stories of Gabriel's rescue of prophets from dire circumstances and invariably is mentioned as hero to the biblical protagonists. Besides delivering verses of revelation to the Prophet Mohammed, Archangel Gabriel consoles Adam after his eviction from Eden, protects Abraham from the fiery kiln, supports Moses in his clash with the illusionists of Egypt, and coaches David to prepare his armor.

Many Christian denominations revere Archangel Gabriel as a saint. Besides Catholicism, Eastern Orthodoxy, Lutheranism, Coptic Christianity, and Anglicanism honor Him.

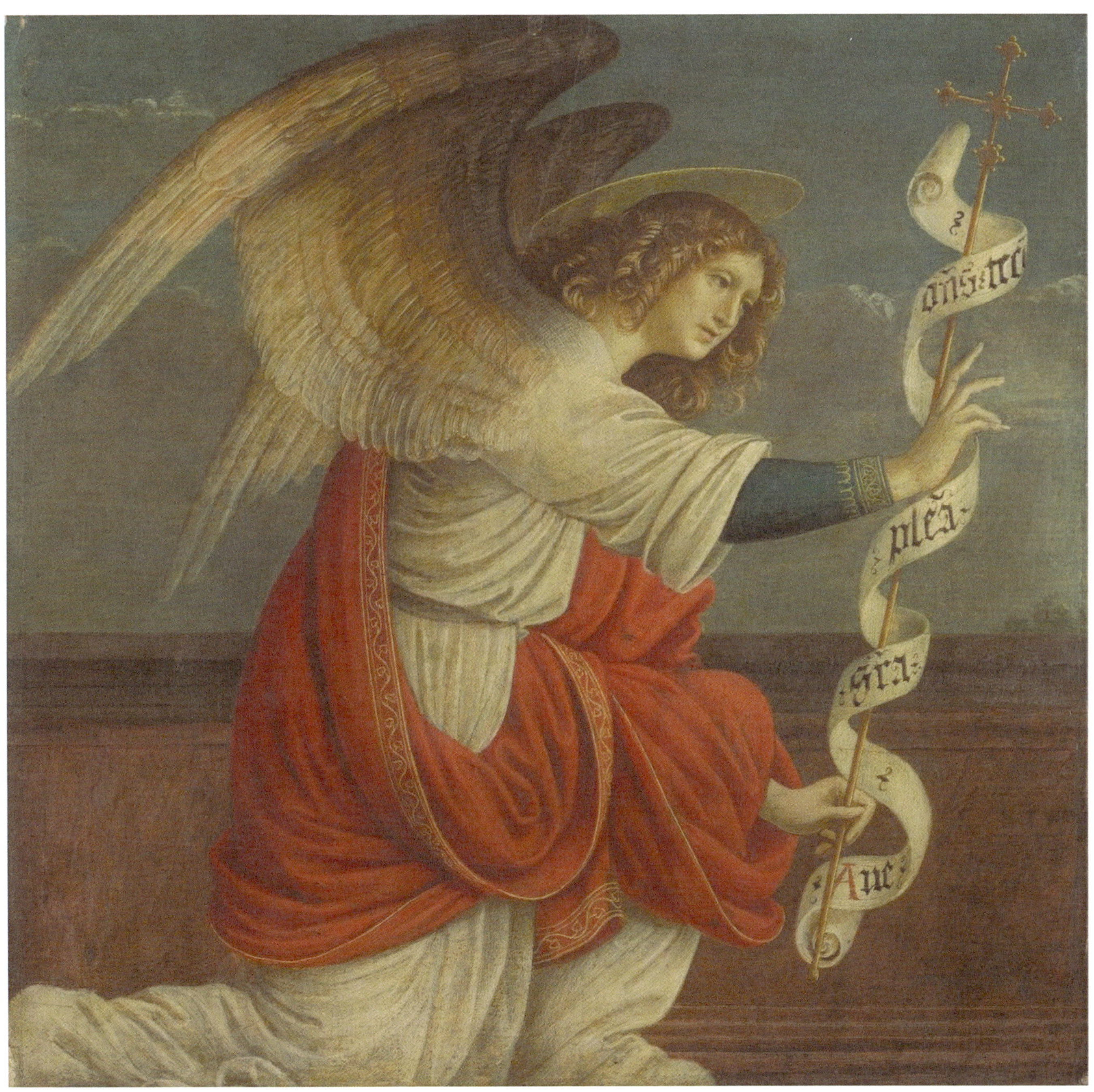


[34] Gaudenzio Ferrari, *The Annunciation: The Angel Gabriel*, 1508-9, The National Gallery, London, *Courtesy Layard Bequest, 1916.* https://www.nationalgallery.org.uk/paintings/gaudenzio-ferrari-the-annunciation-the-angel-gabriel, Accessed 29 January 2025.

# SONNET FOR SAINT GABRIEL THE ARCHANGEL

Our brother Gabriel, the prince *en garde*

From towers where the Holy Palace reigns

Alights the Earth to finish bold campaigns

For flowered he from God, we should regard

Lest evil steal away or we discard

The wisdom from this holy one that deigns

To teach the law that life recedes and gains

And surest route that treks the longest yard


For everywhere the wind was ever freed

The warrior ones have fought to die or slay

But Gabriel's ability will lead

With God in him, no succor shall delay

Nor Paradise forget his living creed

That banishes the evil of the day

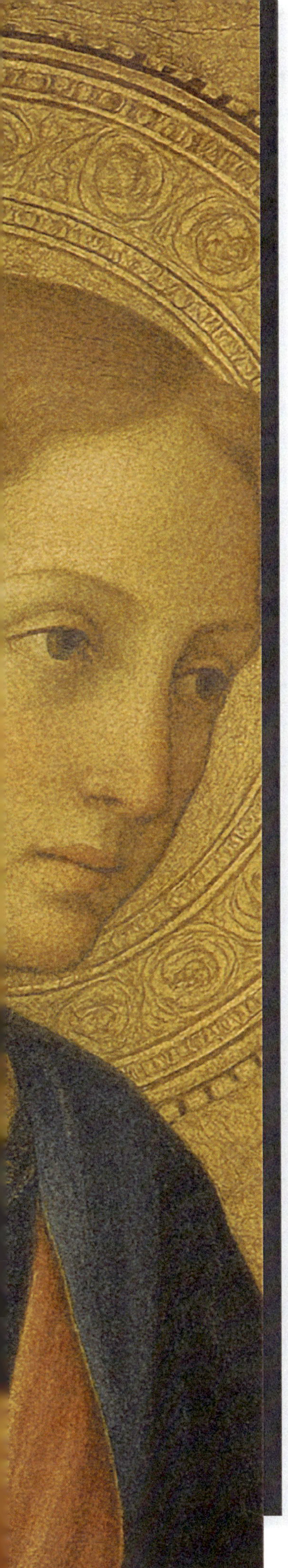



Raphael: "God has healed"

"I am Raphael, one of the seven angels who stand and serve  before the Glory of the Lord." (Tobit 12:15)

"And the second voice I heard blessing the Elect One and the elect ones who hang upon the Lord of Spirits…who is set over all the diseases and all the wounds of the children of men, is Raphael."[35]

All three Abrahamic religions, Judaism, Christianity, and Islam, venerate Saint Raphael. In Christianity the archangel is venerated by the denominations of the Roman Catholic, Eastern Catholic, Eastern Orthodox, Oriental Orthodox, and Lutheran churches, the Anglican Communion, and Methodism.

"Raphael, because of his association with healing, became identified with the unnamed angel of *John 5:1–4* who periodically stirred the pool of Bethesda 'and he that went down first into the pond after the motion of the water was made whole of whatsoever infirmity he lay under'. The Catholic Church accordingly links Raphael with Michael and Gabriel as saints whose intercession can be sought through prayer."[36]

"The Archangel Raphael is said to have appeared in Cordoba, Spain, during the 16th century; in response to the city's appeal, Pope Innocent X allowed the local celebration of a feast in the Archangel's honor on May 7, the date of the principal apparition. Saint John of God, founder of the Hospital order that bears his name, is also said to have received visitations from Saint Raphael, who encouraged and instructed him. In tribute to this, many of the Brothers

[35] *The Complete Book of Enoch.*
[36] Catholic News Agency, *Saints Michael, Gabriel, Raphael, Archangels*, https://www.catholicnewsagency.com/saint/sts-michael-gabriel-raphael-archangels-609, Accessed 14 March 2025.

Hospitallers of St. John of God's facilities are called 'Raphael Centers' to this day. The 18th century Neapolitan nun, Saint Maria Francesca of the Five Wounds, is also said to have seen apparitions of Raphael. On July 8, 1497, when Vasco da Gama set sail from Lisbon with his four-ship fleet to India, the flagship was named *São Rafael* at the insistence of King Manuel I of Portugal. When the flotilla reached the Cape of Good Hope on October 22, the sailors debarked and erected a column in the archangel's honor. The little statue of Raphael that accompanied Da Gama on the voyage is now in the Naval Museum in Lisbon."[37]

About 15 years ago I had a deep emotional wound and a bout with depression at the same time. I went to a naturopathic healer who called upon Archangel Raphael to heal me. I had no idea she was going to do this. The session lasted about an hour. I was relieved by the end of a certain spiritual and physical heaviness. I look back and know I was helped immensely, because after that I rose out of the depression gradually and healed. Working just two times with this gentle healer I became aware of just how helpful the angelic kingdom could be. And I was pointed the way to access, for myself, the higher state of the Holy of Holies within.

[37] Cresswell, Julia, *The Watkins Dictionary of Angels; Archangels*, Watkins Publishing, London, 2012.

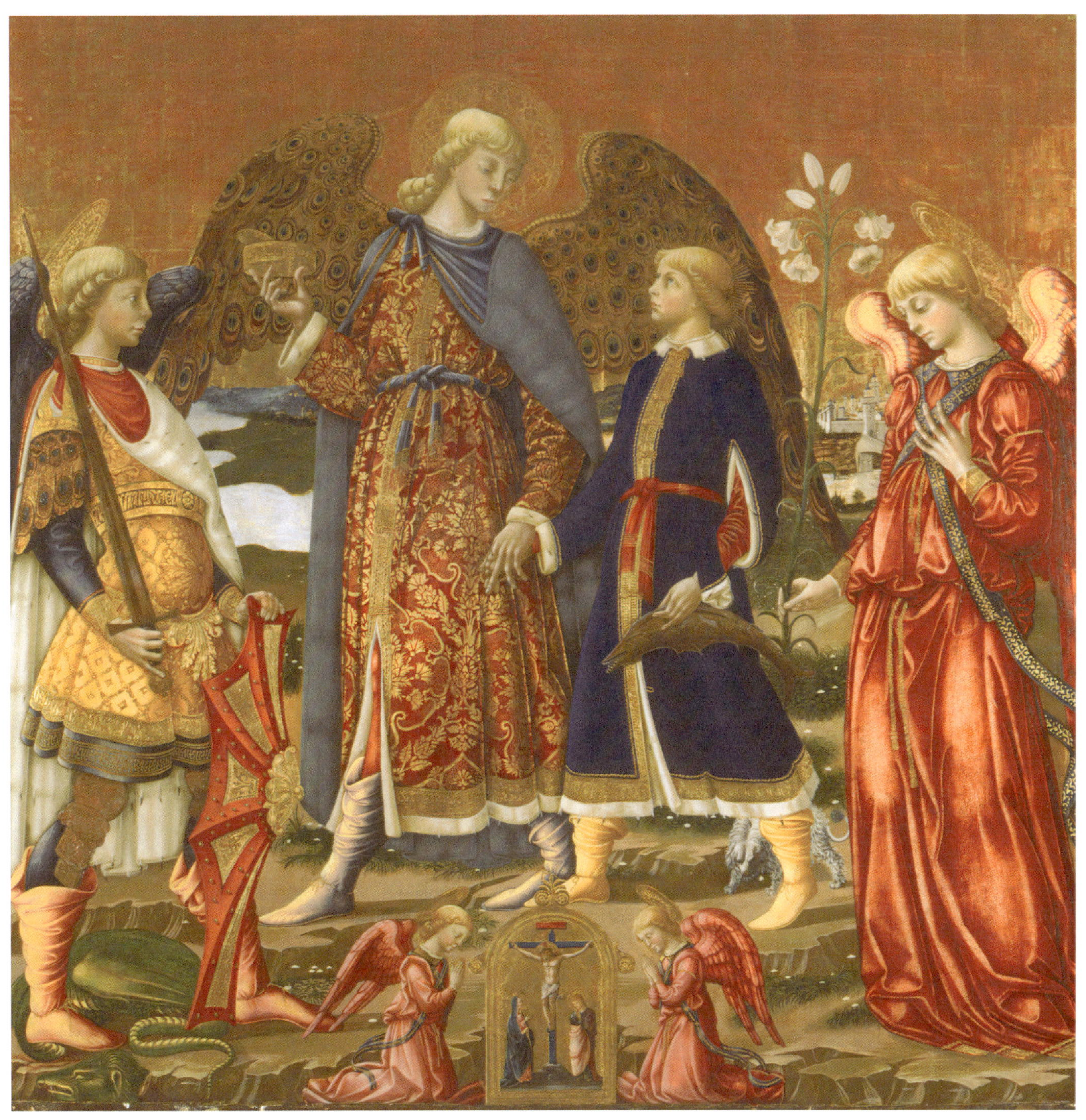

[38] Neri di Bicci, *Tobias and Three Archangels,* 1471, Detroit Institute of Arts, Detroit, *Courtesy Artvee.com.*

# SONNET FOR SAINT RAPHAEL THE ARCHANGEL

When we have soothed the wounds of every clan

The Staff of Life will strike the cask of wine

For holy ones foresee from perch divine

That all must work according to the plan

For pangs of trauma, even from Japan

Appeal to Raphael with hands benign

For he can reconcile what's out of line

The wise Archangel fights like superman


The scaffold of the angels shall reveal

Saint Raphael, with reach from heights beyond

The healed shall know the pure one and his seal

And comfort that releases every bond

When human souls recover all their zeal

My heart he takes, but where shall he abscond?

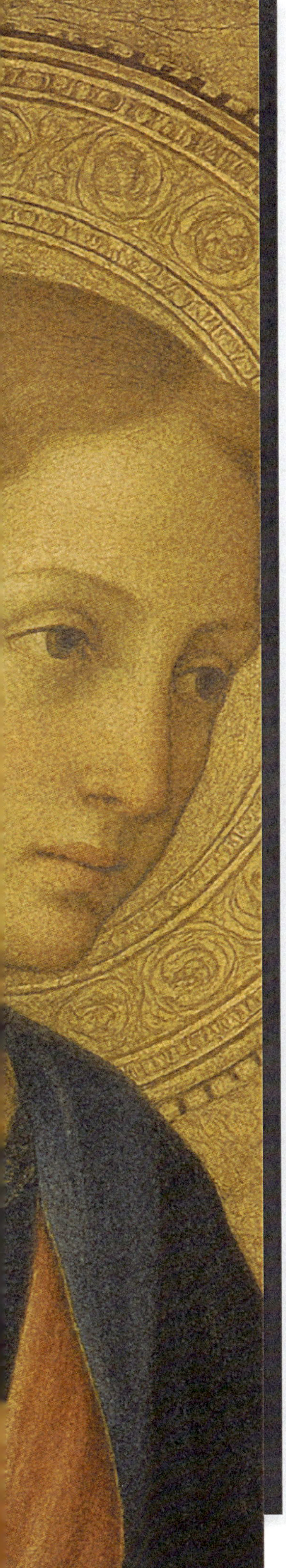



Uriel: "God is my flame."

"Although Archangel Uriel is not mentioned by name in the Bible, he is one of the four angels mentioned in Enoch 4(9):1, the chapter "Intercession of Angels." The others are Michael, Gabriel, and Raphael. Uriel appears in a number of places in the Book of Enoch. Uriel was sent to tell Noah that the earth would be destroyed by a deluge (Enoch 10:1). He describes the angels who had led men into false worship (19:1) and he was assigned to watch over the world and Tartarus (20:2). He prophesies to Enoch that the fallen angels (stars) would be bound and punished for 10,000 years (21:5), and that those who said unseemly things about the Lord would be punished in "the accursed valley" (27:2). He instructs Enoch in the names of the stars, their positions and movements according to their months (33:4), and tells him about the courses of the heavenly luminaries, their relations to each other, and how they regulate the time and condition of the world (72:1); he also discusses the lunar year (74:2) and the movements of the moon (75:3, 4; 78:10; 79:6; 80:1). Uriel is mentioned also in 2 Esdras 4:1, 5:20, 10:28, and he rebuked Esdras for questioning the ways of God by propounding questions that have no answers."[39]

- The Ethiopian Orthodox Church considers 2 Esdras part of their canon.
- The Anglican (Communion) and Coptic Christians of Ethiopia and Eritrea venerate Archangel Uriel with a feast day.

[39] Wikipedia Contributors, *Uriel*, Wikipedia, The Free Encyclopedia, Accessed 2 February 2025. https://en.wikipedia.org/wiki/Uriel.

- "In the 16th century, Archangel Uriel appeared before the Sicilian friar Antonio Lo Duca and told him to build a church in the Termini area. Lo Duca told Pope Pius IV about the apparition, the pope then asked Michelangelo to design the church, which became the Basilica of St. Mary of the Angels and of the Martyrs located at the Esedra Plaza."[40]

[40] "The Story of Uriel, the Forgotten Archangel", *www.romereports.com.* Rome Reports. 27 November 2011. Retrieved 2 February 2025.

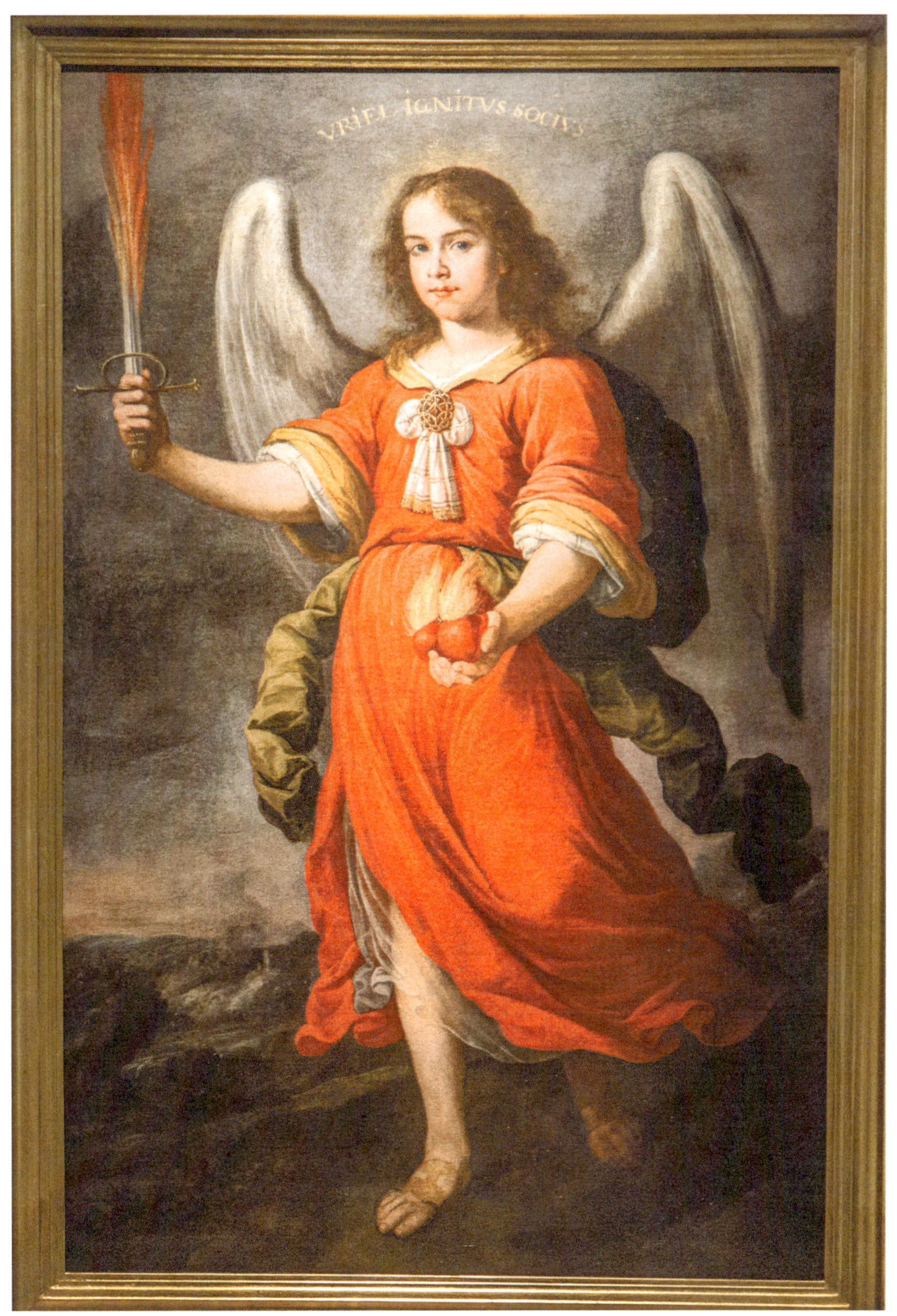


[41] Alonso Miguel Tovar, *Archangel Uriel*, c. 18th Century, The Fine Arts Museum, Seville, Courtesy ID324741663, https://www.dreamstime.com/archangel-uriel-holds-fire-sword-heart-th-century-painting-alonso-miguel-tovar-exhibited-fine-arts-image324741663, © feliperf4_info Felipe Rodriguez.

# SONNET TO SAINT URIEL THE ARCHANGEL

In fires of the wisdom babbles cease

In radiance of rays from sacred isle

Above the clouds and din of human guile

The angels built a palace white as fleece

Whose flaming golden gates with ease release

The utterance of God that none defile

As Uriel bears lilies of the Nile

To children who know not angelic peace


And Uriel, who counts the eminence

Of luminary clusters night unveils

Will teach of revolutions so immense

Arranging orbs in order by their scales

Illuminating us on matter dense

As voyage through forever ever sails

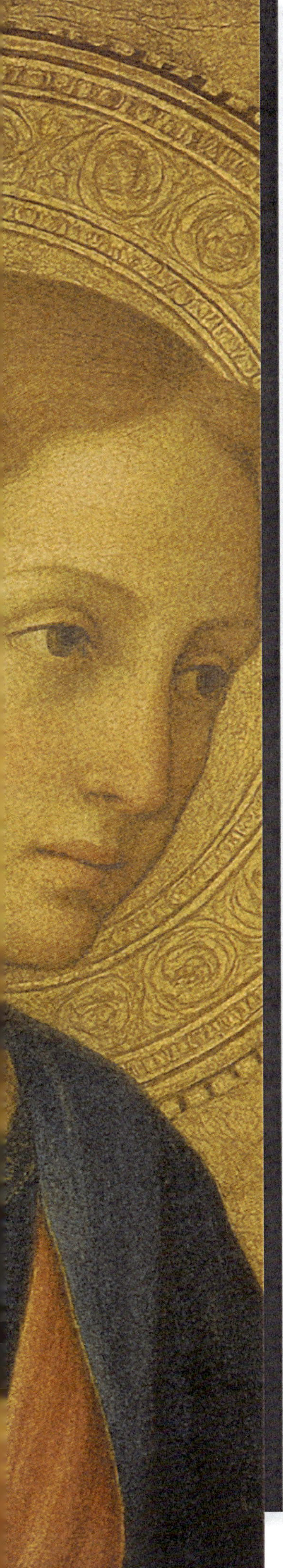



"Angel means 'messenger.' So all the heavenly spirits, so far as they make known Divine things, are called 'angels.' But the superior angels enjoy a certain excellence, as regards this manifestation, from which the superior orders are denominated. The lowest order of angels possess no excellence above the common manifestation; and therefore it is denominated from manifestation only; and thus the common name remains as it were proper to the lowest order, as Dionysius says (Coel. Hier. v). Or we may say that the lowest order can be specially called the order of 'angels,' forasmuch as they announce things to us immediately."[42]

"Such, therefore, are they (angels) who participate first, and in an all-various manner, in Deity, and reveal first, and in many ways, the Divine Mysteries. Wherefore they, above all, are pre-eminently worthy of the name Angel because they first receive the Divine Light, and through them are transmitted to us the revelations which are above us. It is thus that the Law (as it is written in the Scriptures) was given to us by Angels and, both before and after the days of the Law, Angels guided our illustrious forefathers to God, either by declaring to them what they should do and leading them from error and an evil life to the straight path of truth, or by making known to them the Divine Law, or in the manner of interpreters, by showing to them holy Hierarchies, or secret visions of supermundane Mysteries, or certain divine prophecies."[43]

Within this broad group of Angels, there are subdivisions as there are with all the choirs of the hierarchy. Generally speaking there are the White Angels, whose job it is to control the elementals of the air, rivers, seas, and streams. Our Guardian Angels, assigned to every human, evolve from this group. They take

[42] Aquinas, *Summa Theologica, Article 108*.
[43] Dionysius the Areopagite, *The Celestial Hierarchy*.

an oath when becoming our guardian angels, understanding the sanctity of the human soul. This step in their evolution is also the phase where they become self-conscious and experience the "human" phase of growth. Their goal after that service and maturation is to become an archangel. The Green Angels, of which I have not seen, are responsible for protecting and propagating the plant matter of the planet. And the Violet Angels nourish and develop the etheric physical bodies of all living things on the physical plane. The etheric body is the exact replica of the dense physical body only made of finer, etheric matter. Their long-term goal is to become principalities. Those with etheric vision can see the violet auras surrounding the plants and other physical matter. This is the angelic substance of the Violet Angels. Each gradation of angels has a form of service for its development and a goal.

As regards the human contact with angels, there are at least two thoughts to ponder. First, the reason we know what we know about the angelic hierarchy is precisely because there has been human contact with the heavenly messengers. Second, true divine angelic revelations are not inefficiently distributed. In other words, God as represented in our Divine Hierarchies, angelic and human, does not waste energy or mince words.

Lower order spirits abound, incomprehensively so, on the astral planes, which are the emotional planes, and are the closest to the physical plane on which we reside. The contact through the astral plane is not always reliable, in general, because the astral plane is a reflection of the mental planes, and it is colored by the emotional energy of humanity. The resurrected advanced saints reside on the higher mental planes. Suffice to say, there are beings on the astral plane who do God's work. But just because we are contacted by a voice or vision does not mean it is safe to pursue due to the possibility of the innumerable mischief makers and non-profound among the citizens of the astral plane. It is always a good question to ask, "Why am I being contacted?". This is why St. Teresa of Avila and others have wisely cautioned about it. The truer contact is made on the mental plane when in the secret place of the Holy of Holies within, when protected in the Divine Radiance, the holy Light shed by the Most Holy Seraphim. Saint Teresa of Avila calls this the 5th, 6th, and 7th Mansions in her classic book on mysticism, Interior Castles. This is the protecting Light from the City of God, the hallway to the Lord of Spirits within. It is known by other names in every mystical branch of the world's religious cultures.

At times I've been asked how to cultivate a relationship with one's guardian angel or patron saint. I can say this: The Master is the expert. For Christians, that master is normally Master Jesus. Don't forget there are twenty-four Elders surrounding the throne of God as stated in Revelation, and as Jesus stated to his apostles:

> "Amen, I say to you that you who have followed me, in the new age, when the
> Son of Man is seated on his throne of glory, will yourselves sit on twelve thrones,
> judging the twelve tribes of Israel." (Matthew 19:28)

That said, becoming holy is the Way, in any case, whether intending to grow spiritually or contact your guardian angel. The guardian angel is always overwatching, whether we are in conscious contact or not. To elaborate on it, there is nothing that follows which cannot be extracted from the Christian Bible. Here is the ancient training discipline of Christian mystics. The foundation is modeled after Saint John the Baptist (and Elijah before him), then Saint Anthony and the monastics in the deserts of Egypt, to Mount Athos where the Hesychastic practices to gain Theosis (union with God) flourished, to the Benedictines, thence to Saint Enda of Aran Isle and the Celtic monks of the western isles. In truth, the Celts had mysticism in their pre-Christian nature religion, which they naturally translated into the Christian mysticism. The discipline ascends in this order:

*Purification→Illumination→Union with God.*

Another way of saying it: 1) Devotion's aspiration purifies desire by spiritual fire; 2) Spiritual reading leads to mental Illumination; and 3) Complete obedience to the Master demonstrates living by the will of God, creating union with same. The purpose is not to become morally correct, but to eliminate the blockages of negativities within us to open ourselves to the outpouring graces from the Holy Ones.

Forgiveness of all things is part of purifying oneself and becoming humble. Great humility resides latent inside each one us, as does patience and endurance, the longing for wisdom and truth, love, compassion, unselfishness, energy, calm, strength, faithfulness, intuition, clear intelligence, and serene temper. These are all qualities of the Christ.

The process of purification is a long road, as any priest or religious will tell you. Conversion to living a saintly life is not an overnight success. It can take one's whole life. One should pray, and pray, and pray with the heart until it is an automatic activity, dare I say discipline, in one's life. Laying it all out to God every day, all the unholy actions and thoughts, works to clear the conscience and the negative wall they set up to block the grace of God. This is also an aspect of the design of the Sacrament of Reconciliation. Opening the heart and being totally honest in prayer is paramount because otherwise we are dishonest with ourselves. This is one reason for the Catholic devotion of the Sacred Heart of Jesus and the Immaculate Heart of Mary. If prayer flows through the heart, it is linked to and passes through the soul, the sacred sheath of the image of God within us.

Eventually one arrives at the admission that we know next to nothing about God. Few people have seen the Most High God, the Lord of the World, as the Prophet Isaiah did in a vision when the Seraphim purified his lips with a hot ember. On the other hand, if one has seen actual God, one is not allowed to talk about it. We are within Creation and depend on God, within Whom "we live and move and have our being." We are hidden with Christ in God, so our absolute nature as a pure spirit is a mystery to us. We don't and can't know our absolute being via the five senses. We have to go beyond the five senses to get a clue as to Who God is and whom we are. We have seen the Master Jesus and so we've seen an aspect of God in human form, but we can never know the totality of God while we are here on Earth. The human mind, being finite, cannot conceive of the entirety of our infinite God. Acknowledging in humility our ignorance of God, it follows that our capacity for humility increases.

Another step is the practice of honesty in our minds, and sincerity through our hearts. This learned behavior will simplify many things in life, because one will start to *think, say,* and *do* the same thing, aligning with and living the truth. This will nurture a heart-centered life blended with reason. Wisdom blended with Love. An all-too-common behavior is to say one thing, think another, and do yet another, different from the other two. We are not living the truth in union with our soul in that approach. We become fractionalized in our integrity. And our integrity is all that we really have. Recall that the angelic kingdom is based on the unity of oneness.

Prayer, again, as an everyday practice is important. There is a point at which the devotional nature of the disciple leads to meditation or contemplation. This is a complementary interior path to the exterior life. An interior life is required to travel the road that Jesus demonstrated with His life. Just look at what He did by finding a quiet place away from the crowds to pray. It was done much more often than is noted in the Gospels. "Be still and know that I am God" says the psalmist. The combination of prayer and meditation is powerful for one's growth in the experience of God. The two other avenues in addition to, not in place of the latter, are the paths of knowledge or wisdom and service to others. Since it is not likely that one who seeks God will meet God, in this physical world, it is "a pearl of great price" to experience God within. "The kingdom of heaven is within you" is the guidance from the Master Jesus. Meditation is the avenue par excellence to experience God within. The image of God, the Holy Spirit, is stamped in our own soul. In fact, the soul's "body" is simply a vehicle for that image of God, just as our physical body is a vehicle for the soul on this physical plane. Saint Paul iterates this principle a number of times. Leave all things of this world at the door, including the ego of the personality, and go within. This is the only approach that I know of to access our own innate divinity "down here" on Earth. There are a number of good books on Christian meditation for edification and instruction. Mysticism, the inner path of direct divine experience, is not an option, it is a natural "next step" as one grows spiritually. Spiritual growth also requires this paradox: All that is seen which most people perceive as real, must be perceived by the seeker as the unreal; and all the things that are invisible and to most seem unreal, the seeker must see as real with a longing for the eternal, which is unseen, and the true and higher reality. And to achieve the sanctity or holiness required, as Thomas Merton taught, "…all sanctity depends on renunciation, detachment, and self-denial. But self-denial does not end when we have given up all our deliberate faults and imperfections."

The disciple will be contacted when it is determined that he or she is ready. Walking the path of compassion to God requires growth in sanctity which attracts the benevolent helpers. Guardian angels are always willing to guide us. There is no preparation or "having to be good enough" for their loving, selfless guidance. Even a person at rock bottom in sin can turn to their guardian angel for succor. We only need to cleanse and open our hearts and minds to Them to become closer. Developing one's own intuition to discern the inner messages from the soul and the guardian angel takes time. Developing intuition is another reason for the journey of the inner path. The sky is the limit for spiritual contact with the Master. What Master Jesus and Mother Mary can enable us to do is beyond our comprehension. Every step we take toward God multiplies the movement of the divine assistance towards us. The man or woman needs simply to take action. Dreaming about it and putting it off is a glamor of the emotions or illusion of the mind.

The first time I was awakened that my prayers were being heard was when I was about 30 years old, early in my Air Force vocation. I was praying in a small room in my house at 1 a.m. I usually said prayers, then meditated for an hour while the house was completely quiet. After the first phrase of the prayers starting with, "O my God, please hear my prayer", a spiritual "lightning bolt" shot through me, with a spiritual electrical charge that jolted me backwards from my kneeling position. After that experience, the reality kicked in that our angels and saints on the other side await us to take a step toward God.

Contact with the Master happens when He needs us to do something, and He assesses we are ready to serve the Plan of God usefully. The Master won't waste time with us if we're not ready, so His direct contact means he knows we're ready. This doesn't mean He is not trying to help us through life behind the scenes. So you may not even be aware about the Master's influence. As we step along the spiritual path, we are first aspirants, then on a probationary phase of the path of discipleship. The holy influence behind the scene may instigate a feeling very strongly about getting involved in something altruistic, starting a spiritual discipline, or getting down to business about something that you've been putting off. No matter, there is no time wasted in God's plan once the person decides to enter the spiritual path, and all is done in perfect time.

The perfect architect efficiently and wisely guides the disciple's progression spiritually. Said another way, we humans are the only ones who waste time as far as spiritual growth is concerned. The baggage of our attachments to "things" of this material world, and negative emotions of the lower astral/emotional part of our makeup, are usually what hold us back. The less we carry, the faster and higher we can go, by the grace of God.

Admonition from the Blessed Mother Mary to her spiritual disciple, Venerable Maria of Agreda:

> "I wish thee to understand well, how by the ministry of these angels, mortals would receive great enlightenment, and incomparable favors from the Lord, if only they did not hinder them by their sins and abominations, and by their oblivion of this inestimable blessing. But as they block up the way, which God in his ineffable Providence has opened up for conducting them to eternal felicity, the greater part of them damn themselves, whereas, with the

protection of the angels and with a proper estimate of his blessing, they could save themselves."[44]

The ultimate spiritual goal is Union with God, Salvation, Enlightenment, The Fullness of Joy, Nirvana, and Self-realization, all different words for the same attainment. There is no trophy to collect. And there is no attainment in *anything* without divine grace. Another reason to be humble in our approach. We live in a sea of divine mercy, should we only become aware of it. We can experience the spiritual gift of salvation, even if momentarily in contemplative awareness, while living on Earth.

Henceforth, I encourage the reader to befriend your guardian angel through holy prayer to build a relationship that you may together happily walk with God. This can be a precious part of life on Earth that cannot be taken away. We each contain the Holy Spirit in our souls as a birthright, as sons and daughters bearing the image of God. The Sacrament of Baptism invokes it. Then pray in the Holy Spirit, from your heart which is connected to your soul, to the guardian angel dedicated to your welfare.

The bottom line for the seeker: to become a mystic of devotion and a disciple of wisdom to grow in sanctity is the plight of Christian effort; however it is not the goal, only the plight. Union is the goal. Living in contemplation, if you will. We don't have to go anywhere to find God and His eternal Holy Ones. The layers of spiritual planes where they reside completely surround us. It is we who block their impressions and guidance with wrong thoughts, emotions, and actions. The work of purification—pure food, pure mind, and constant devotion to God—is designed to eliminate our blockages to our spiritual benefactors, angels and saints, who serve the Godhead. And it clears the path to our own soul which rests "hidden with Christ", Who embodies or ensouls every soul on this planet.

[44] Mary of Jesus of Agreda, *Mystical City of God,* Translated by Rev. George J. Blatter, W. B. Conkey Company, Hammond, Indiana, 1914.

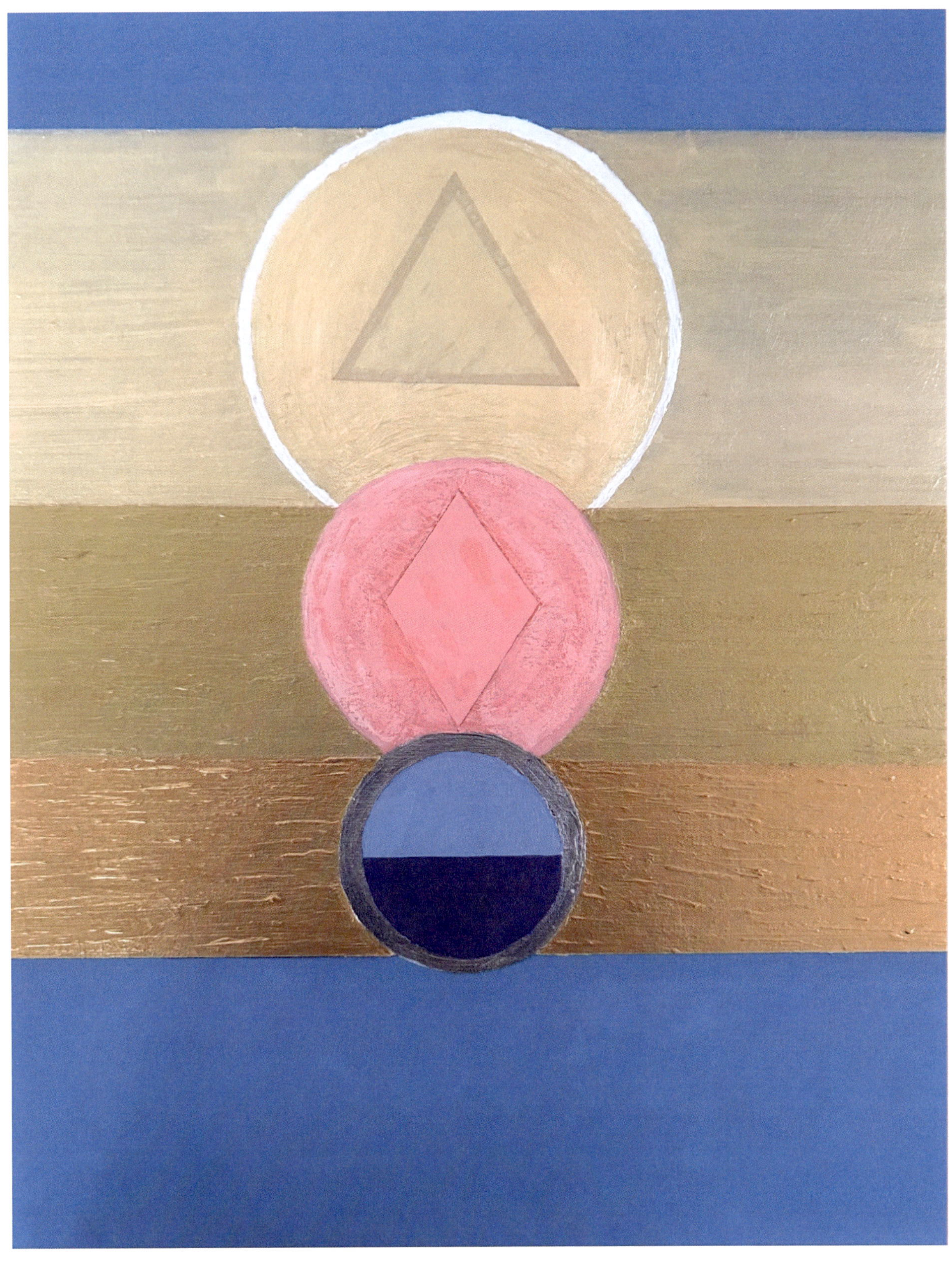

For Christians, the bottom blue section represents the material cosmos where the meditator is located in the world of matter and thus duality. The bottom circle shows the meditator joined spiritually to a patron saint, an advanced disciple of the Master Jesus, who transmits and steps down the spiritual fire during contemplation to the disciple. The rose-colored circle denotes the Blessed Mother, with the diamond symbol of spiritual initiation, to which she guides the "little one" on the journey of discipleship. The top gold circle represents Christ consciousness, or Holy of Holies, of the soul in union with the attendant Holy Trinity symbolized by the triangle. This is where the Master Jesus steps down the spiritual fire to the Blessed Mother. Gold is symbolically the color of the divine and grows finer in higher vibration as consciousness elevates, ringed in white by the purity of mind.

# SONNET TO THE MOST HOLY ANGELS

From love of God there comes a sweet affair

When harmless actions fortress any heart

With purity, humility, to start

As everything in life connects with prayer

The angels let us know that they are there

The inner life and outer life make art

Of living in a world that seems apart

From all the realms the angels build with care


Our source in God is One, a simple math

No origin without its holy other

The boulders in the world may block the path

Yet we must find the spring of Holy Mother

When Spirit-Matter sanctified this bath

The angels poured the water as our brother

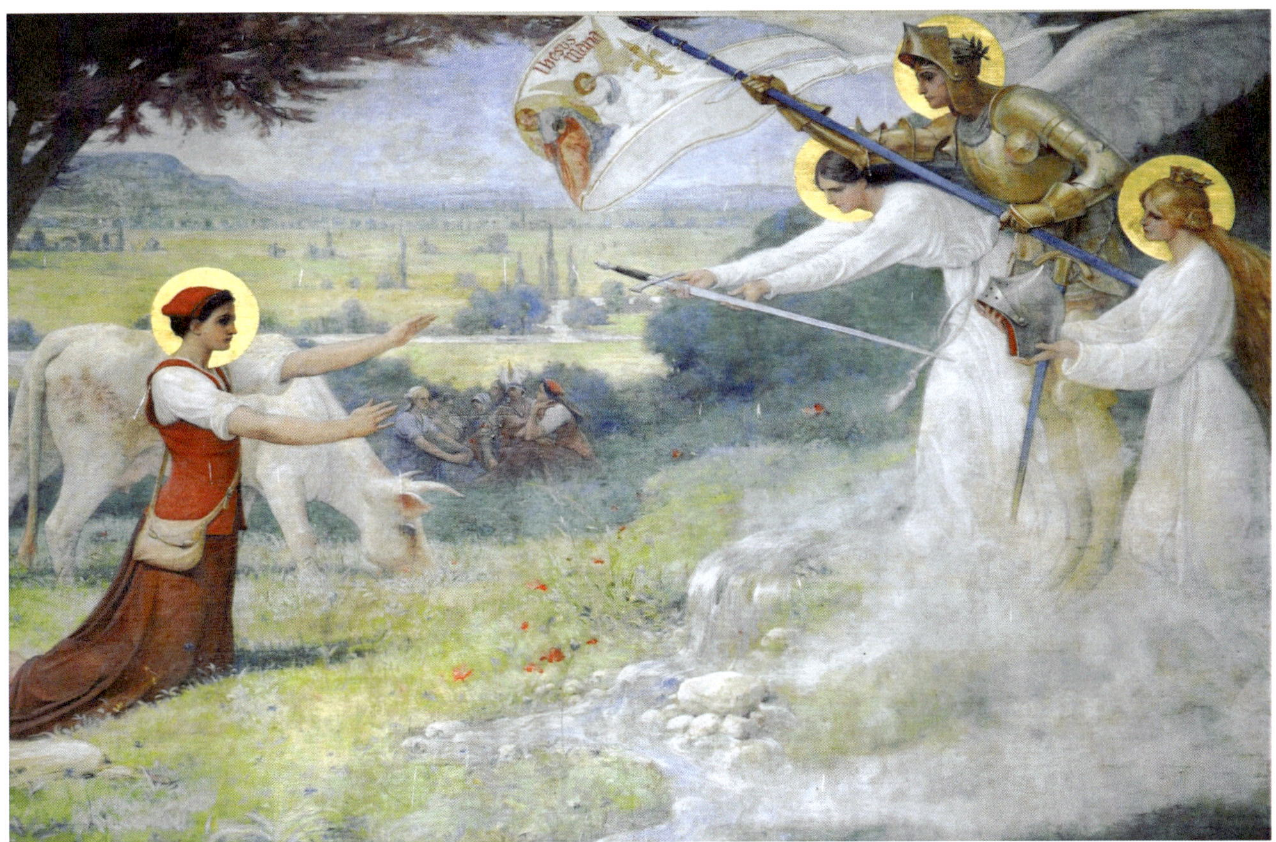



SAINT JOAN'S CONNECTION TO the angels transpired throughout her life. It is recorded that she said she was influenced most by Saint Michael the Archangel, Saint Catherine of Alexandria, and Saint Margaret.

[45] Lionel Noel Royer, *Scene de la Vie de Jeanne D'Arc*, 1913, Basilica of Bois-Chenu, Domremy, France, *Courtesy DPA Picture-Alliance.*

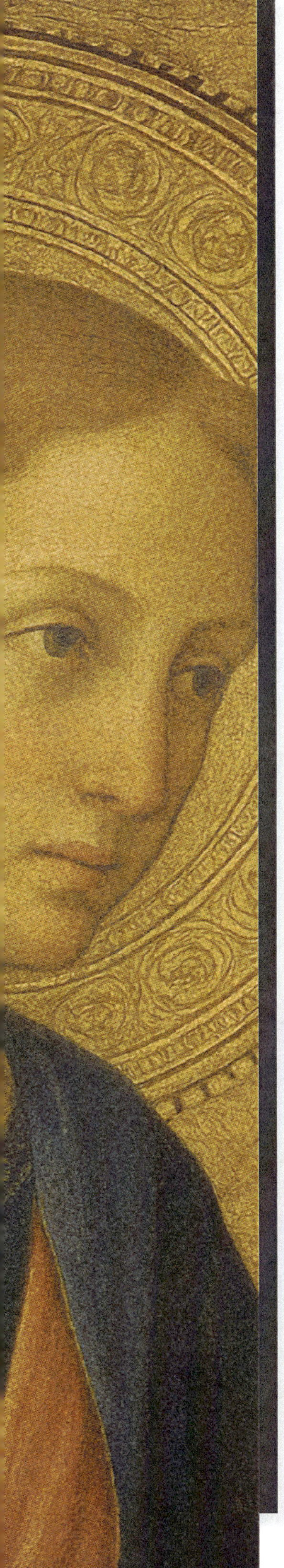

<h1 style="text-align:center">A SHORT TREATISE OF THE HOLY ANGELS<br>ON CREATION</h1>

*I*n April of 2021 I was living near the beach in a studio rental apartment while searching for a house. I received a message in meditation in my little space from the holy angels: "Continue to come to the beach so we can talk to you there." I had been seeing the White Angels and elementals who are responsible for the air and seas during my evening strolls to the water with increasing presence and movements, so magical in their ethereal bodies hovering over the waves. I returned to the beach that evening to sit and watch the sunset and the magnificent creation before me. As the sun began to fall into the sea at the horizon, I calmed my mind and began to see the angelic movements and etheric plane elementals and energies. I heard a holy angel speak to me telepathically.

"What you see here before you is the quintessential example in Nature of the aspects of God which you've come to know as the Holy Being of Eternity, the Holy Cosmos, the representation or symbol of Time and sacred Becoming of the Logos. Eternity, which you know stands silently before God, engulfs the Cosmos and all within it, as this ocean engulfs your gaze and the entire planet. The Cosmos, and all the angels assigned within it, toil day and night to glorify the Creation of the One Most Holy God. The angels of the clouds, of the great waters, of the earth, and even from the light of the Sun, bring the unity and oneness of the entire biosphere into harmony, perpetually so that one day even mankind will join us in glorifying our creator. When man (man…from Sanskrit: 'the thinker') in his mortal form recognizes this, we the angelic hierarchy will be finally acting as One with souls of mortal man."

"Nowhere else is it so apparent than at the seashore that you can witness the relationship of Time to the Cosmos. The relentless waves recurring, over and over, as does Time, lapping in its periodic recurrences, witnessing to Eternity, and cleansing (the soil and air) in the white foam from the thrashing waters onto the shore, purifying and evolving all through Time. This is the Creator's medium for the Becoming of all sentient and non-sentient life within the Holy Cosmos, the universal (Cosmic) Son of God. Here again, the Cosmos is one with Eternity, and Time is one with the Cosmos and its Becoming."

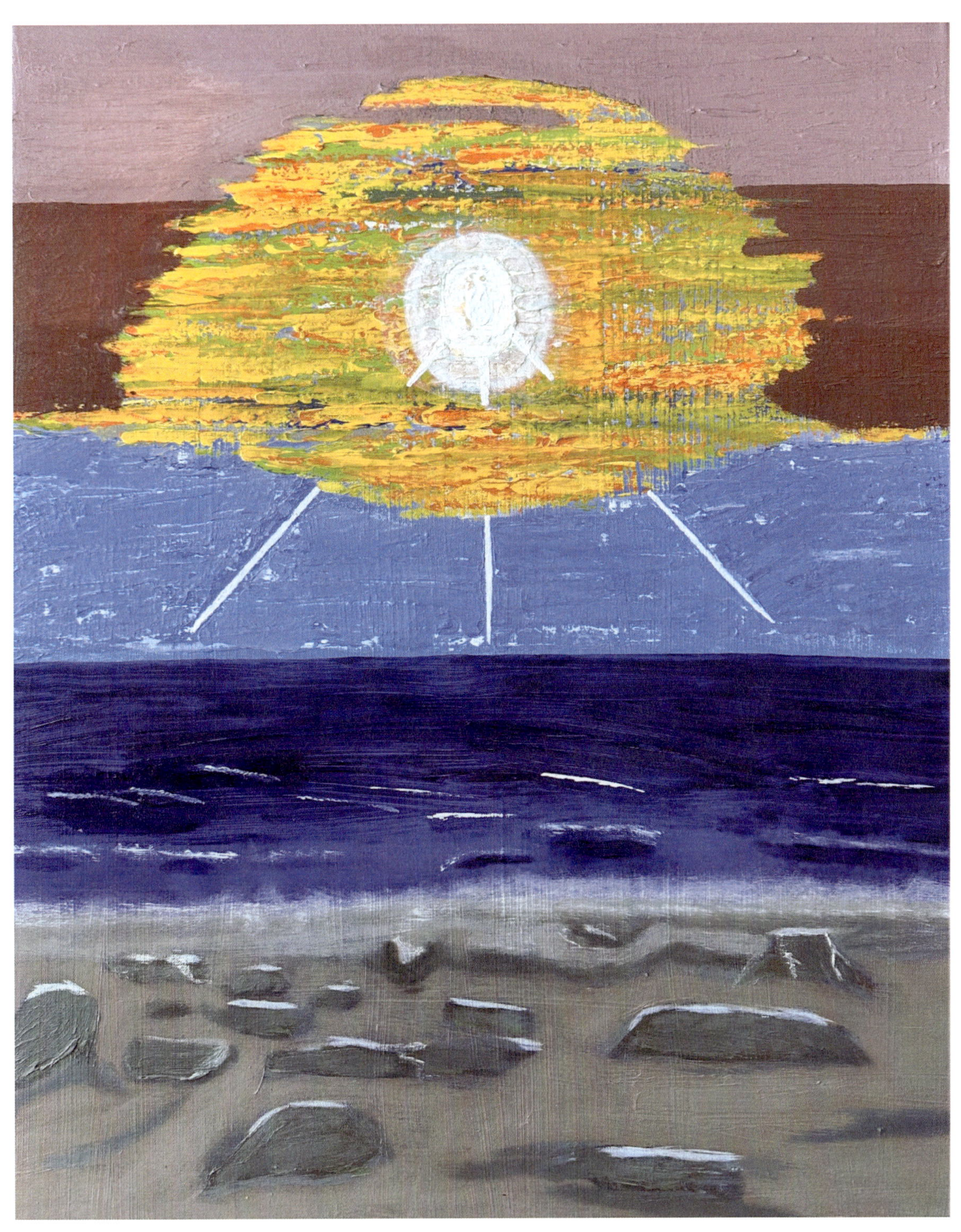

THE FIVE ELEMENTS ARE Earth, Water, Air, Fire, and Aether. The fifth element of Aether was philosophically established by Plato and his student Aristotle in the 6th Century B.C. and is represented by the dark and light violet colors. In reality, it permeates everything. The White Angel in the center is working its divine duties over the air and water, enshrouded by the Sun's solar fire. Aether, as part of the physical plane, consists of the finer matter above the gaseous state which science has begun to detect, most notably via Kirlian photography. The White Angels and Elementals are seen in the etheric level of matter.

GUARDIAN ANGEL

My true and blessed friend behind the veil
Who casts a shaft of mysteries aflame
You sacrifice your life to guide and heal
And weather all the foibles I shall claim
In youth beguiled, I sat in darkness drowned
Imprisoned in a nightmare and its throes
Awakened by a wind of light I found
The company of angels you disclose

That once ago the dust of demon's fray
Would jolt me into prayer upon my knees
Dimensions of a world without dismay
Displayed celestial lights of floating seas
And then a friend I knew not was my own
Allowed the view that gifts the heart to see
The flight of angels white as light that shone
On hallowed way that guides and shadows me

# THE CLOUDS

The clouds, they wander, whipped by light-beamed reins

Like camels with no master and no rest

Befriending angels, wind and sun and sea

Who bridle life—unfurling every test

Wherein they fade, then whirl their sudden spree

In silken cloaks that boast of hidden plains

IN THIS LATEST POETICAL adventure into Christian Mysticism, Ronnie Smith has devotedly researched the angelic hierarchy. He follows the winding trail through the mystical and cosmological concepts of the ancient Chaldeans and Babylonians, to Judaism, and eventually into Christianity. He reveals to the public in this book his mystical encounters throughout his life that offer insights into the angelic kingdom not often considered. The author grew up in Chicago, Illinois and Baltimore, Maryland. He earned a bachelor's degree at Loyola College, now Loyola University Maryland, and later studied engineering at the University of Maryland. Colonel Smith retired from the Air Force after thirty years of service, where he commanded or flew over 1,000 flights over Antarctica as well as serving in Air Force/U.N. missions on all the other continents. In his extended deployments to Antarctica, a vast desert continent of glacial ice and snow, he discovered contemplation and divine majesty. His poetry and paintings rest upon the foundation of the underlying wonder of God in humanity and creation. He hopes to develop a spiritual retreat to allow seekers to reconnect to their own holy God-centered soul, experienced in a sanctuary of the divine natural world. Ronnie is also an acolyte in the Catholic Church.